The Guitarist's Bookshelf

A practical music encyclopedia for today's versatile guitarist.

by Amy Appleby and Peter Pickow

With special thanks to Carl Ruebel, Jr. for editorial assistance

Cover photography by Randal Wallace

Order No. AM 961543
US International Standard Book Number: 0.8256.1772.3
UK International Standard Book Number: 0.7119.7903.0

Exclusive Distributors:
Music Sales Corporation
257 Park Avenue South, New York, NY 10010 USA
Music Sales Limited
8/9 Frith Street, London W1V 5TZ England
Music Sales Pty. Limited
120 Rothschild Street, Rosebery, Sydney, NSW 2018, Australia

Printed in the United States of America by
Vicks Lithograph and Printing Corporation

N

Madrid

Contents

Book 2: Music Theory for Guitarists   35

Book 4: Guitar Chord Dictionary   137

 # Book 1

Guitar Owner's Manual

There are a dazzling variety of guitars in the world today—and dozens of different musical genres that feature acoustic and electric guitar. In the hands of different musicians, these instruments are able to produce a wide range of distinctive sounds and effects. In this book, you'll find an introduction to the important members of the guitar family. Here you will also find instructions on restringing and tuning your guitar, as well as some practical advice on routine instrument care and repair.

The Guitar Family

Whether you have an acoustic or an electric guitar, the principles of playing are fundamentally the same. So are most of the physical features of both instruments. This section provides an overview of the guitars commonly used today.

To learn about chords and tunings for the standard guitar, refer to *Book 4: Guitar Chord Dictionary.* Chords and tunings for specialty guitars and related instruments are provided in *Book 5: Guitarist's Guide to Other Fretted Instruments.*

Section Contents

Acoustic Guitars

The guitar has a rich musical history spanning five centuries. Its widespread popularity is largely due to the fact that it is portable and easy to play. Today, the guitar is used by both classical and contemporary musicians—and is an integral part of the music of many cultures. With a range of over three octaves, the guitar is a expressive and versatile instrument, called by Beethoven a "miniature orchestra." Acoustic guitars come in a variety of shapes and sizes, but they all share the same basic characteristics shown in the diagram at right.

The first guitars had strings made from animal sinew (commonly called *cat gut*). Today, acoustic guitars can be divided into two basic categories: *nylon-string* and *steel-string*. As these terms imply, the basic difference lies in the type of strings used. There are also major structural differences. A nylon-string guitar should never be strung with steel strings, and vice versa. For instructions on stringing these guitars, see the following section, "Stringing the Guitar."

Nylon-String

The nylon-string guitar is commonly used for classical music, soft folk, and certain kinds of jazz and Latin music. Most beginners start with nylon-string guitars because the strings are lighter and easier to fret. The neck of the nylon-string guitar is wide, allowing left-hand fingers more room to move. This type of guitar is also generally less expensive than a steel-string guitar of comparable quality.

Steel-String

The steel-string guitar is well suited to contemporary folk music, bluegrass, country, and blues. This type of guitar is louder than the nylon-string guitar—and can sustain a note longer. This makes the steel-string guitar useful in a band situation either as a rhythm or lead instrument. The neck of the steel-string guitar is generally longer than that of the nylon-string guitar. This makes it easier to play in the higher positions.

Twelve-String

The twelve-string guitar has a full, rich sound that can be heard in many popular venues. This type of guitar has six pairs of strings—and each pair is called a *course*. The lower courses are tuned in octaves. The strings in each of the two highest courses are tuned to the same pitch (in unison). Each course is picked and fretted as if it were one string. Because the twelve-string guitar is more difficult to play and tune than a six-string guitar, it is not usually a good choice for beginners.

Pickups

There are several different types of devices that allow you to electronically amplify an acoustic guitar. For steel-string guitars, there are magnetic pickups similar to those built-in to electric guitars. Various pickups and microphones are also available for nylon-string guitars. Many of today's acoustic guitars come with a built-in pickup system which includes EQ and volume controls, as well as a handy output socket. A microphone-style pickup is shown in the diagram below.

The Parts of the Acoustic Guitar

	Steel-String Guitar	Nylon-String Guitar
Neck	usually 14 frets until joining body	12 frets until joining body
	approximately 1¾ inches wide	approximately 2 inches wide
	usually has a reinforcing steel truss rod	traditionally made without a truss rod
Body	usually slightly bigger than a classical guitar	approximately 19 inches long and 15 inches wide (at the widest point)
Peghead	often has a shield-shaped plastic plate to cover the tip of the truss rod	
	solid peghead with covered or "worm-and-gear" tuning machines	slotted peghead with barrel-type tuning machines
Bridge	has bridge pins or tailpiece to secure strings	strings are tied to bridge

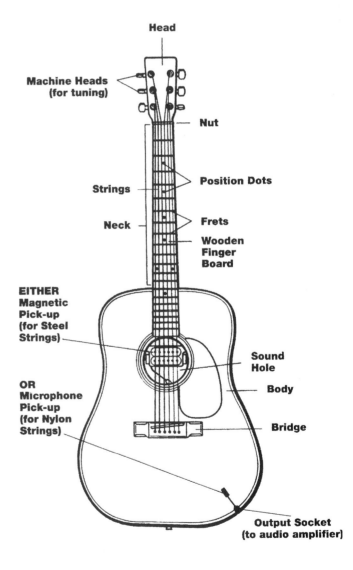

Electric Guitars

Throughout the 1920s and 1930s, guitarists searched for a way to be heard above the brass and woodwinds of the popular dance band. During this time, acoustic guitarists experimented with microphones and contact pickups. The real breakthrough was the development of the magnetic pickup, which translates the actual vibration of the guitar's steel strings into an audio signal which can be sent to an amplifier.

Guitar designers realized that an instrument with a magnetic pickup didn't need a large, resonant body to produce sound. They found that a solid-body guitar can actually sustain notes longer than a hollow-body guitar. Thus the modern electric solid-body guitar was born. Hollow-body and semihollow-body electric guitars remain popular to this day due to their distinctive and expressive tonal range.

Although there are literally thousands of different shapes and styles of electric guitar available today, they all share the same basic characteristics shown in the diagram at right.

Solid-Body

The solid-body electric guitar has been the mainstay of rock, pop, R&B, country, and blues music for decades—and it is by far the most popular type of electric guitar used today. All use steel strings and have necks and bodies made of wood, plastic, metal, or composite materials. All have built-in electronics to create an audio signal, an output jack, and volume control. Some have additional features, including active tone control, stereo outputs, multiple pickups, and pickup selector switches.

Hollow-Body

An electric guitar with a resonant, hollow body produces a traditional, warm sound. For this reason, the hollow-body electric guitar is favored by musicians who play jazz, blues, and country swing. Hollow-body electric guitars usually have a carved archtop which gives them a characteristic punchy acoustic sound, even when they are not amplified. When unplugged, the hollow-body electric guitar makes an excellent acoustic guitar.

Semihollow-Body

This type of guitar offers a compromise between the solid-body and hollow-body guitar. Although its body is actually hollow, it is much shallower than a true hollow-body guitar. The semihollow-body guitar still produces some of the warm, resonant sound of the hollow-body guitar. However, the shallower body allows for more sustain—and cuts down on inherent feedback problems when playing at high volumes.

The Parts of the Electric Guitar

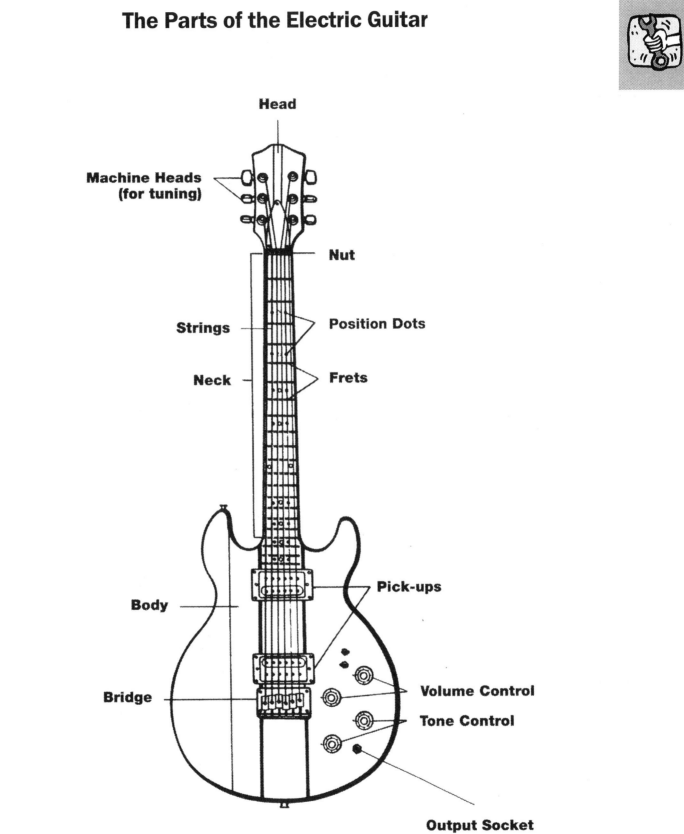

Head

Machine Heads
(for tuning)

Nut

Strings

Position Dots

Neck

Frets

Pick-ups

Body

Bridge

Volume Control

Tone Control

Output Socket
(to audio amplifier)

MIDI Guitars

MIDI is an acronym for *Musical Instrument Digital Interface* (pronounced "middy"). Designed by a world committee, this universal computer language allows MIDI-compatible devices to exchange and store musical information in a precise digital format. At first, MIDI was used primarily for keyboard instruments and sequencers. Now almost any instrument can be set up to send MIDI information. This allows guitarists, wind players, drummers, and even vocalists to control a synthesizer and create a wide variety of musical effects beyond the range of their individual instruments.

Manufacturers offer both acoustic and electric guitars with built-in interfaces. These are both referred to as *MIDI guitars*. However, any guitar can be retrofitted to send MIDI data using a MIDI pickup.

The first MIDI guitars were not really guitars, but rather MIDI controllers shaped like guitars. Some used elaborate switches and sensors built in to the neck or frets, others required using strings the gauge of a high E string for all six strings. With advances in computer music technology, it became possible to build a normal guitar with a special *hex pickup* to transmit MIDI data. The hex pickup is really six individual pickups—one for each string—in a single unit. Most often, the data is sent in a proprietary format over a special cable to a decoder, which then outputs standard MIDI data that can control a synth. There are also specially designed synths that can accept data directly from the hex pickup. In other systems, the decoder is built in to the guitar, so that the instrument's MIDI output may be plugged directly in to a synth or sequencer.

Specialty Guitars

Stringed instruments have existed for thousands of years—and guitar-like instruments date back at least as far as the Renaissance. Today, there are several related instruments that guitarists find relatively easy to master. These include the tenor guitar, baritone guitar, bass guitar, and instruments in the ukulele family. Tunings for these instruments are found in *Book 5: Guitarist's Guide to Other Fretted Instruments*. Here you will also find information on how to adapt the chords listed in the section "Chords in Standard Tuning" in *Book 4: Guitar Chord Dictionary*.

Other instruments in the guitar family include the lap steel and Dobro (or Hawaiian guitar). Specific chords and tunings for these instruments are provided in *Book 5: Guitarist's Guide to Other Fretted Instruments*.

Related Instruments

Instruments in the banjo and mandolin families are closely related to the guitar, and are also easy for the average guitarist to learn quickly. Specific chords and tunings for several of these related instruments are provided in *Book 5: Guitarist's Guide to Other Fretted Instruments*.

Stringing the Guitar

This section provides instructions on stringing a nylon-string or steel-string acoustic guitar. Instructions are also provided for stringing a standard electric guitar. For information on tuning, see the following section.

Section Contents

When to Change Strings

If you play regularly, you'll probably want to put new strings on your guitar every four to six months. If you play a lot, you may need to change them as often as once a week. In any case, you can tell when you need to restring your guitar by its sound. Old strings can make your tone sound muffled, dead, or even off-pitch. Dirt or rust is also sometimes visible on old steel strings.

In the end, your ear is your best guide when it comes to deciding when to replace your guitar strings. If your tone sounds bright and clear, it's not necessary to replace the strings on your guitar. If it sounds dull, it's probably time to change. It's a good idea to keep an extra set of strings in your guitar case so you can replace strings quickly and easily when necessary. If a string breaks, it's probably an indication that it's time to replace the entire set.

Removing Old Strings

Whether you have a nylon-string or steel-string guitar, it's important to remove your old strings with care. Don't be tempted to cut off all the strings at once. Instead, remove them one at a time to protect the neck of your guitar from unnecessary stress. In fact, many guitarists like to replace each string before removing the next. This is probably a good idea with older guitars, as it minimizes the strain put on the neck and body by the string-changing process.

First loosen the tuning peg to release the tension, then cut the string with a scissor (for nylon strings) or wire cutter (for steel strings). Repeat this procedure to remove the remaining strings. Remember that the tips of steel strings can be quite sharp, so take care not to cut yourself when removing these.

After you have removed all the old strings, take the time to wipe the fretboard with a clean cloth that is slightly damp. Then wipe off any excess moisture with a dry cloth.

Nylon Strings

As a general rule, nylon strings are all pretty much the same. However, some manufacturers do offer different string *tensions,* ranging from low to high. Although the high-tension strings may not necessarily be thicker than low-tension strings, they do have more density. This requires additional string tension, which makes them a bit louder than low-tension strings—and a bit harder to play.

Steel Strings

Steel-string acoustic guitars and electric guitars all require steel strings. These come in different weights called *gauges*. The gauges of the strings affect the relative volume and tone of the sound produced. The thicker the string, the more volume it can produce. Heavier gauge strings require more tension than lighter gauge strings, and are harder to play. They also put more stress on the neck, bridge, top, and braces of your guitar.

Guitarists often refer to the overall weight of a set of strings in terms of the gauge of the first, or high E, string. Although the gauges of the individual strings in a set vary from one manufacturer to the next, you can get a good idea of the standard gauges available for steel-string acoustic and electric guitars from the following comparison chart. The numbers in parentheses refer to the gauge of the first string in millimeters.

Gauges of Steel Strings

Acoustic Guitar

medium (.013)
light (.012)
extra-light (.010 or .011)

Electric Guitar

medium (.011)
light (.009)
extra-light (.008)

A Word on Stringing

On a standard acoustic guitar, strings are matched to the tuning machines in a circle, from lowest to highest, as shown in the diagram at right.

Here are a few tips to remember when you are stringing an acoustic guitar:

Use the right type of strings for your instrument: nylon for a nylon-string guitar and steel for a steel-string guitar.

Match each string to the appropriate notches on the bridge and nut.

Don't clip strings to length before putting them on. Tighten them and bring them up to pitch before cutting off any excess.

Avoid putting any kinks or bends in the strings.

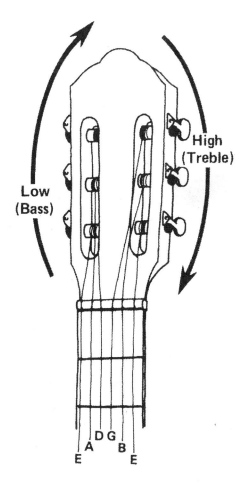

Replacing Nylon Strings

Nylon-string guitars have a simple type of bridge to which the individual strings are tied. Note that some manufacturers produce *ball-end* nylon strings, which have a small *ball* or *barrel* attached to one end of each string. If you have a set of these strings, there is no need to tie the strings to the bridge; just pass the plain end of each string through the appropriate hole in the bridge and skip to the third step.

Insert the end of the string into the proper hole of the bridge and pull it through until about 1½ to 2 inches sticks out the other side. Pass this short end of the string back over the bridge, and then under the main part of the string.

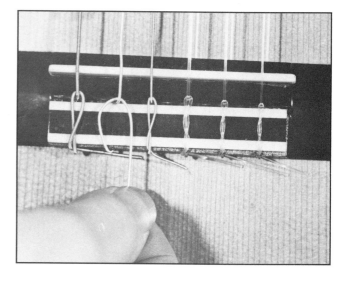

Now pass the short end of the string back over and then under itself to form a loose loop. This loop should resemble a figure eight, as shown at right. (For the top three strings, pass the short end of the string over and then under itself a second time to create a double knot.) Then pull gently, but firmly, on the long end of the string to tighten the knot.

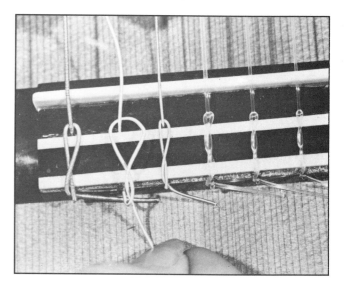

Thread the string through the hole in the tuning-machine *barrel* from front to rear. Bring the end around the upper side of the barrel and back to the front. Loop the free end around the string as shown at right, and pull it back again.

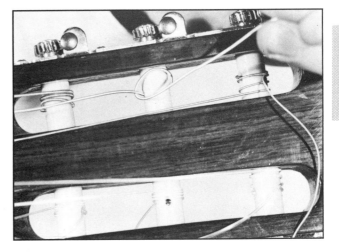

Tune the string until you are sure it won't slip. When the string is tuned up to pitch, there should be at least two full windings on the barrel. Cut both ends of the string fairly short (leave about ¼ inch) to avoid buzzes and rattles. Be sure to wind all strings so that the tuning machines turn in the proper direction. As you face the back of the peghead, the tuning pegs should turn counterclockwise for the string to get tighter.

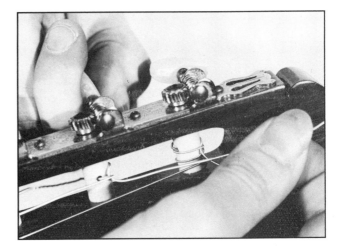

Replacing Steel Strings

On both acoustic and electric guitars the strings are attached to the *machine heads* on one end and to the *bridge* at the other. When restringing your guitar, you should always be careful to avoid getting any bends or kinks in the new strings. Take care when uncoiling and handling the new strings, as the tips can be very sharp.

Acoustic and electric steel-string guitars are all pretty much the same at the head-stock end, but there are several variations on the way that the strings are attached to the instrument's other end. Most acoustic steel-string guitars have a bridge with *bridge pins.* If your guitar has a row of small plastic pins along the bridge, you can skip ahead to the "Replacing Strings on a Guitar with Bridge Pins," on the adjacent page. If your guitar has a tailpiece, read the following paragraphs and then skip to the second step on the adjacent page.

Restringing a Tailpiece Guitar

All solid-body electric guitars and some acoustic guitars have some type of *tailpiece bridge.* On acoustic guitars, the tailpiece is often anchored to the strap button at the bottom of the instrument. This type of tailpiece is called a *trapeze tailpiece.* There are many other varieties of tailpiece-type bridges, including *stop-tailpieces, tremolo bridges, locking-tremolo bridges,* and so on.

Several types of tailpiece bridges for electric guitars are shown below. With some tailpiece bridges, the ball end of the string fits into a notch in the tailpiece. With other types, you must pass the string up through a hole in the body of the guitar. Certain high-tech tremolo bridges may require the use of a special tool to remove and replace the strings. Before removing any strings, examine carefully how they are attached to your particular type of tailpiece. Remove and replace strings one at a time, so that you will always have a model to copy.

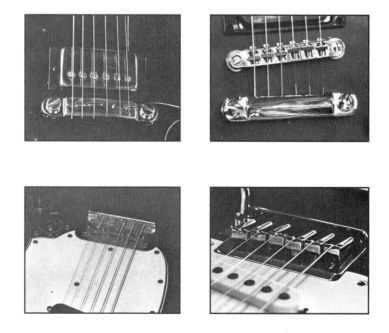

Restringing a Guitar with Bridge Pins

To get the old string off, loosen it completely, then gently push it back into its hole. At this point you should be able to remove the bridge pin. If you have trouble getting the pin out, you can use a screwdriver or a coin to gently pry it loose. Just be sure to use an adjacent bridge pin as a fulcrum, rather than the bridge itself, to avoid damaging the wood.

Put the ball end of the new string into the correct hole. Insert the bridge pin so that the grooved side faces the string. The slot and the tension created by tuning will be enough to secure the string. For now, tug gently on the long end of the string to make sure that it is snugly in place.

Thread the string straight through the hole in the appropriate tuning-machine post at the head of the guitar. Gently bring the free end halfway around the post: clockwise for the bass strings and counterclockwise for the treble strings.

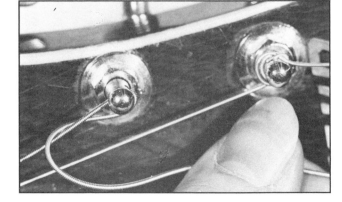

Loop the free end of the string under the longer part and bend it back gently. As the string is tightened, this loop will lock it in place and prevent it from slipping. When the string is in tune, there should be at least one winding around the post. Cut this end of the string fairly short (leave about ¼ inch) to avoid buzzes and rattles.

Tuning the Guitar

Whether you're playing a gig or practicing at home, you will always sound your best when your instrument is well tuned. In a group setting, it's important that musicians can tune quickly and accurately—and maintain good tuning throughout the session. This section provides complete instructions on tuning your guitar using three common methods.

You can find alternate tunings and chords for guitar in "Chords in Open Tunings" in *Book 4: Guitar Chord Dictionary.* Chords and tunings for specialty guitars and guitar-related instruments are provided in ***Book 5: Guitarist's Guide to Other Fretted Instruments.***

Section Contents

Relative Tuning

If your guitar is already pretty well in tune, you can use the relative tuning method to tune up. You can tune each string of the guitar to its correct pitch by turning the appropriate *tuning peg.*

- Use a left-hand finger to press down on the sixth string (low E) just behind (to the left of) the fifth fret. When you pluck this string, you will hear an A note. This note should sound the same as the fifth string played *open* (that is, without being fretted by a left-hand finger).

- If the fifth string (or A string) does not sound in tune, use the tuning peg to loosen it until it sounds lower than the sixth string, fifth fret. Then slowly bring it up to pitch.

- When your A string is in tune, fret it at the fifth fret. This note is D, and should sound the same as the open D, or fourth, string.

- When your D string is in tune, fret it at the fifth fret. This note is G, and should sound the same as the open G, or third, string.

- When your G string is in tune, fret it at the fourth fret. This note is B, and should sound the same as the open B, or second, string.

- When your B string is in tune, fret it at the fifth fret. This note is E, and should sound the same as the open high E, or first, string.

This diagram summarizes the relative tuning method.

Relative Tuning Method

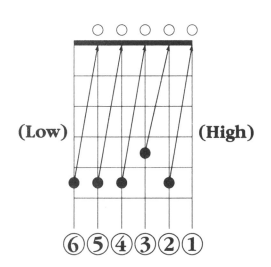

Tuning to a Piano

You can use a piano or electronic keyboard instrument to tune each string of your guitar. If you are tuning to an acoustic piano, it's naturally important that the piano itself is well tuned.

Here are the notes on the keyboard that correspond to the open strings of the guitar. These notes represent the actual sounds of the guitar strings. However, music for guitar is written one octave higher than it sounds to make it easier to read.

Tuning to a Piano

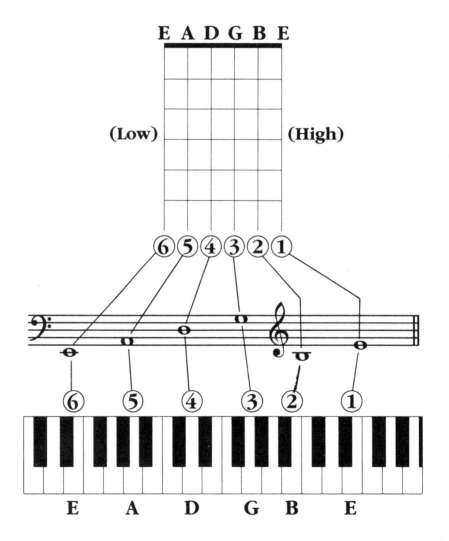

Tuning by Harmonics

Harmonics are tones produced without actually fretting a string. The easiest harmonics to sound are those produced by touching the strings at the twelfth fret.

To play harmonics, just touch a string lightly with a left-hand finger directly above the fret indicated. Then pluck the string with your right-hand index or middle finger and remove the left-hand finger from the string immediately. The result is a high, bell-like tone. For this reason, harmonics are often referred to as *chimes*.

Like the relative tuning method, this method can only help you get your guitar in tune to itself. If you are playing with other people, you will need to need to tune at least one of your strings to one of the other instruments before applying this tuning method.

- Assuming that your low E (sixth) string is in tune, sound the harmonic at the fifth fret. This tone (E) should sound the same as the harmonic on the A (fifth) string, seventh fret. If the two tones are not perfectly in tune, loosen the A string until it sounds lower, and then slowly bring it up to pitch.

- When your A string is in tune, sound its harmonic at the fifth fret. Compare and match this tone (A) to the harmonic on the D (fourth) string, seventh fret.

- When your D string is in tune, sound its harmonic at the fifth fret. Compare and match this tone (D) to the harmonic on the G (third) string, seventh fret.

- To tune the B (second) string, sound the harmonic at the seventh fret of the low E (sixth) string. Compare and match this tone (B) to the open B (second) string.

- To tune the high E (first) string, sound the harmonic at the fifth fret of the low E (sixth) string. Compare and match this tone (E) to the open high E (first) string.

Guitar Care and Repair

Most guitars don't require much in the way of special care. In fact, if you treat it right, a good guitar should last a lifetime. In this section, you will find some valuable advice on maintaining your instrument, some tips on storage and travel, and an overview of the most common guitar repairs. There are also descriptions of popular guitar accessories that can help extend the life of your instrument or make it easier to play.

Section Contents

Cases

Like other instruments, the guitar should always be stored and transported in a case. The least expensive case is a plastic cover with a zipper known as a *gig bag*. This type of case will protect your instrument from dirt and moisture—and prevent most nicks and scratches. However, they offer little real protection against bangs and bumps which may occur during travel. Cardboard cases offer more protection and additional space to carry accessories. There are also high-quality, padded gig bags made of leather, canvas, or nylon which offer a significantly higher level of protection than the simple plastic variety.

Semi-hardshell cases are made from thin wood or fiberboard. This shell is covered with high-grade vinyl, and occasionally there is padding between the wood and the vinyl cover. The inside is usually lined with a soft material, allowing the guitar to rest snugly and not bang around while it is being carried.

Hardshell cases are similar to the semi-hardshell. The hardshell case is made from thicker wood (usually ½-inch plywood) and thus offers more protection. Moreover, the inside is often more thickly padded than the semi-hardshell case. Although the hardshell case offers more than adequate protection under almost any circumstances, its main drawback is that it is heavy. Some companies make fiberglass cases which are extremely protective, but weigh comparatively less. As the quality of the case increases, so does the quality of the hardware (latches, hinges, and handles). Most cases have one latch that locks. While this lock cannot prevent theft, it can discourage the uninvited borrower.

No matter what kind of case you have, make sure that your guitar fits snugly inside. Rattling around in a case that fits loosely can at least knock a guitar out of tune, and may eventually lead to more serious problems. If you cannot find a case that is a perfect fit for your instrument, use a towel or a clean, soft rag for padding. This is especially necessary in cardboard cases, or any other case that does not have padding built in.

At home, many guitarists like to leave their instrument out of the case. Don't invite a costly fall by leaning your instrument up against the furniture or wall. Instead, purchase a guitar stand to keep your instrument safe, yet accessible.

Travel

If you travel a lot with your guitar, you really should use a hardshell or semi-hardshell case. This should protect your instrument from the inevitable dings and cracks that can occur during transit. If you are traveling by car, don't leave your guitar in the trunk for extended periods of time. In the summer, a car trunk will heat up like a small oven. In winter, the trunk can expose an instrument to excessive cold. When you bring an instrument in from the cold, let it warm up gradually in the case for twenty minutes or so before taking it out and playing.

The baggage compartment of an airplane is subject to changes in temperature and air pressure that can cause string tension to rip the bridge off a guitar—or warp and/or crack its neck or face. Before traveling by plane, loosen all the strings of your guitar until they sag. You might also want to consider insuring your instrument. It is not advisable to check an expensive guitar as baggage.

Storage

A guitar is basically made of wood and glue, so anything that can damage these materials can damage your instrument. Avoid storing your guitar in any environment characterized by extremes of heat, cold, dryness, and/or moisture. If you plan to store your guitar for several months, you should probably first loosen all the strings until they sag.

If you live where there is central heating in winter, beware of dryness. Keep an eye out for gaps in the bridge or neck, and consider buying a humidifier. Immediately wipe off any perspiration or moisture from the guitar. Use a soft, clean cloth and rub gently with the grain.

Nicks and scratches on the surface of your guitar do not affect the sound of the instrument. However, they can affect the resale value. Expensive guitars can be insured—usually in a rider to an existing homeowner's insurance policy.

Cleaning

You should clean and polish your guitar periodically. This improves the physical beauty of the instrument and helps to preserve and protect its wood finish. Use lemon oil, boiled linseed oil, or guitar polish. You may wish to use a polish made or endorsed by the company that makes your guitar.

Use a soft, damp cloth to polish your guitar. For a thorough job, take off the strings and rub down the neck as well. This will get ride of the buildup of dirt and oil that can accumulate, and may even affect intonation. Don't use commercial furniture polishes with silicones or other synthetic additives. These may dull or even ruin your instrument's finish. Be sure to wipe off excess polish or oil with a clean cloth.

Lubrication

You should periodically lubricate open tuning machines (called *worm-and-gear*). Put a small amount of petroleum jelly on the end of a toothpick, and insert it in the gears. Use very little lubricant, and wipe off any excess which may attract dust and dirt.

Repairs

If your instrument starts to rattle or buzz when you play it, or if it won't stay in tune, or if it sounds out of tune when you play at certain positions up the neck, it may be in need of some repair. Repairs to the body and neck of a guitar are best left to the professional repairperson. Still, it is a good idea to be familiar with the causes of these problems so that you can talk intelligently with whomever you choose to entrust your instrument to. In addition to getting an estimate before agreeing to let someone work on your guitar, be sure that you understand specifically what the repairperson intends to do to the instrument. Do not be afraid to ask questions and be informed. If someone tells you something that doesn't sound quite right, don't hesitate to get a second opinion.

Initially, whatever repairs you are likely to need will be simple ones—easily affordable and easily accomplished by the staff of your local music store. As you gain more experience (and your instrument gets older), you may realize the need for more extensive repairs or adjustments. Keep in mind that the cost of a major repair—such as refretting or resetting the neck—may actually exceed the value of the instrument. At this point you may find it more prudent to invest in a better guitar.

What follows is an overview of the most common guitar-repair situations. Some of these problems you can fix yourself with standard household tools if you are fairly handy. At any rate, you will find some valuable tips to help you determine just what is wrong with your guitar before you take it in to the shop.

The Frets

If you hear a buzz when you play your instrument, it may be because it has a loose fret. Check each fret, one by one, by pressing one end of the fret down with your finger and then letting go to see if there is any movement. Do this on both sides of the fret. Since you sometimes have to press quite hard, you might want to use the point of a pliers (or similar instrument that is not too sharp). Be careful not to damage the fretboard as you check for loose frets.

If you find a loose fret, you can repair it yourself pretty easily. First place your guitar on its side so that the loose end of the fret is on top. Now press the loose end to the fingerboard with your plier point and let one drop of "Krazy Glue" (or similar type of cyanoacrylate "super glue") run down between the fret and board. Press the fret down for a few minutes while the glue dries. If you get any glue on your skin or tools, you can remove it using acetone (nail polish remover). Never apply acetone to your guitar, as it will dissolve the finish. If you do get glue on the side of the fingerboard, you can sand it off using very fine (600 grit) sandpaper.

If none of your frets are loose, but you still hear string buzzes, this may mean that some of the frets are worn or uneven. In this case the frets must be *dressed*, or filed to make them even. In extreme cases, as with older guitars that have seen a lot of use, it may be necessary to replace the frets.

The Neck

It's very important that the neck of your guitar is in good condition and that it is properly fused to the body. To check for a loose neck, first grab the neck of the guitar near the heel (base) and grab the body of the guitar with the other hand. Then twist your hands in opposite directions to see if there is any movement at the joint. If so, the neck should be repaired. With electric Fenders and other guitars with bolt-on necks, this problem can be easily fixed. However, a loose neck is a major repair for an acoustic guitar, and can be rather expensive. A guitar with a warped (twisted) neck is almost impossible to repair satisfactorily.

To check the straightness of your guitar's neck, first loosen all the strings. Then place the guitar on a table and lay a straightedge lengthwise along the neck to determine if it has a concave or convex bow. If the neck is bowed, you may be able to correct it by adjusting the *truss rod* (see below). If your guitar doesn't have a truss rod, you will have to take it to a professional repairperson for a "heatset," in which the neck is heated and clamped to correct the bow.

If the neck is straight, the next thing to check is whether it is set properly in relation to the body. On some electric guitars with glued-on necks, the neck should slant back at about a five-degree angle in relation to the face of the guitar. On acoustic guitars and electric guitars with bolt-on necks, the neck should be parallel to the face of the guitar. Sight down the fingerboard (not the tops of the frets) from the peghead end. If the neck is attached at the proper angle, your sightline should hit the bridge about one or two millimeters (0.04 to 0.05 inches) below its top. (This distance may be a bit more on classical guitars.) If this distance is more than two millimeters, the neck may have to be reset. This is easily accomplished on a guitar with a bolt-on neck by using a shim made of wood, plastic, or cardboard. On a guitar with a glued-on neck, such as most acoustic guitars, this may be a very involved repair or may not be possible at all.

A truss rod is a steel rod put in the neck for reinforcement. It does not adjust the angle of how the neck is fixed to the guitar body. The truss rod can only straighten the neck between the nut and the twelfth or fourteenth fret. Necks that have an adjustable truss rod have a nut screwed on a rod sticking out on one end of the neck. Most often you will find this in the headstock under a little cover plate (for instance, on Gibson guitars). You may also find it on the other end of the neck, as in the case of many Fender guitars. On some acoustic guitars, the truss rod nut is located inside the body and must be accessed through the sound hole.

A neck with a concave bend may be corrected by turning the truss rod nut clockwise using the proper wrench. For a convex neck, turn the nut counterclockwise. Check your straightedge after every quarter turn to determine if the neck is straight. Unless you are absolutely sure what you are doing, you should never turn the truss-rod nut more than half or three-quarters of a turn in either direction. Overtightening or over-loosening the truss-rod adjustment could cause serious damage to the instrument.

The Tuning Machines

If you hear a rattling noise when you play your guitar, it may originate from the tuning machines. First check that the small setscrews in the ends of the pegs are not loose. Note that over-tightening this screw may make the peg difficult or impossible to turn; just tighten them until they are snug to avoid rattles. The next parts to check are the nuts that go over the tuning peg on the face of the peghead. These may be tightened with a standard pair of pliers, taking care not to scratch the peghead. If all of the setscrews and peg nuts are tight, check the small screws on the back of the peghead that fasten the machines to the peghead. Take care not to over-tighten these screws, because if you strip the screwholes you will worsen the very problem you are trying to remedy.

Another cause of rattling is loose string ends vibrating against the peghead. This is easily fixed by snipping off the excess with a pair of wire cutters. On classical guitars, also check the bridge ends of the strings to make sure that they are not vibrating against the face.

The Finish

Many of the less expensive guitars have a polyurethane finish. This can be a problem if you want to do a touch-up job, since the new finish won't blend in with the old. In this event, even the most expert touch-up will reveal a "ghost line" at best. You won't have that problem with guitars that have the conventional lacquer finishes. New lacquer will blend invisibly with old lacquer. If you do not have experience refinishing instruments, you should leave this job to the professionals.

The Body

It's important that an acoustic guitar has a perfectly straight top. Check to see that the top is not slightly swollen behind the bridge. If it is swollen, the chances are good that it is concave in front of the bridge. If this is the case, it could be that one or more braces or the bridge plate is loose. To check for this, take a small inspection mirror and a flashlight and look through the sound hole at the braces and bridge plate as you press down firmly on the swollen top. If the braces move, the swell can probably be corrected by professional regluing. If you cannot locate a loose brace or bridge plate, then it's possible that the guitar is not repairable.

Cracks and warping in the body of the guitar must be corrected by a professional, which can be rather expensive. Be sure to compare the cost of such a repair to the cost of purchasing a new instrument of similar or better quality.

Accessories

There are dozens of accessories available to the guitarist. These may increase the versatility of the instrument or make it easier to maintain or play. The most common accessories are listed below. To learn more about other guitar accessories or keep abreast of new products, periodically browse music supply catalogs and music stores.

Capos

A capo fits over the neck of the guitar and presses down on the strings at any fret. In this way, it allows the guitarist to change keys without learning a complete set of new chord forms. The capo makes it easy to sing in a comfortable range or play with other musicians in challenging keys. Capos come in a number of different styles. Although the all-metal spring-type capo is preferred for its strength, some guitarists feel they scratch the back of the guitar's neck. The most common capo is the elastic-band type. A single-band capo is used for a nylon-string guitar, while a double-band capo is used for the steel-string guitar.

Humidifiers

Many nylon-string guitarists use a portable humidifier to protect their instruments from dryness, particularly during the winter. (Humidifiers are not recommended for steel-string guitars, as external humidity will cause the strings to rust.) The humidifier can prevent cracking and warping brought on by indoor heating or a desert climate. A commercial guitar humidifier is basically a sponge in a rubber sheath which clips on to the sound hole. This comes with a color-coded card that gauges the humidity. If you would prefer to make your own guitar humidifier, first take a small plastic container or sturdy plastic bag and perforate the top with small holes. Insert a slightly damp sponge and keep it in your case. Occasionally check the sponge to ensure that it is not too dry or damp.

Peg Winders

If you change strings frequently, this inexpensive accessory is an invaluable tool. One end of the peg winder is a hollow cup that fits over the tuning peg. The other end is a handle. Together they form a crank that makes the job of winding and unwinding strings considerably easier and quicker.

Tuning Aids

There are several accessories available that help the guitarist tune with speed and accuracy. The tuning fork provides a single tone to start off the tuning process. An E or A tuning fork is best for tuning the standard guitar. The pitch pipe provides all tones in the chromatic scale. Electronic tuners are the most expensive of all tuning aids. These not only provide any desired pitch, they also evaluate the pitch you play and indicate whether or not it is in tune. When it comes to choosing a tuning device, most guitarists select one that fits easily in the accessories compartment of their guitar case.

Picks

Many non-classical guitarists rely on picks to create a characteristic playing style. Picks are an important accessory for many steel-string guitarists who play rock, folk, bluegrass, blues, or jazz.

There are basically two types of picks: *flatpicks* and *fingerpicks*. All help the player to create a sound with more volume and bite. The most common type of flatpick is a plastic triangle with rounded edges. This type of pick comes in three different thicknesses: light, medium, and heavy. Generally speaking, the lighter-weight picks are used for single melody-line (lead) playing, while heavy picks are reserved for rhythm.

Fingerpicks are used by folk and old-time blues guitarists who play in the fingerpicking style. If you would like to explore this style, use a plastic thumbpick and three metal fingerpicks. The fingerpicks should be put on so the metal curves with the pad of your finger. Some guitarists use only a thumbpick to take advantage of the rich bass sound it produces.

Straps

If you perform in public, it's a good idea to have a guitar strap. This accessory allows the guitarist to stand and move about the stage with ease. These come in a wide range of colors, styles, and prices.

In order to put a strap on your guitar, the instrument must have at least one *strap button* at the very bottom of its body. The other end of the strap may either be attached to another strap button near the neck of the guitar or tied to the peghead, above the nut and under the strings.

Most nylon-string guitars are made without strap buttons. There are special straps that go around the bottom of the guitar and hook into the sound hole to support the instrument. This kind of strap is adequate for occasional use—but if you want to play standing up on a regular basis, you should have a professional repairperson install one or two strap buttons so that you can use a conventional guitar strap.

Stands

If you like to leave your guitar out of its case and ready to play, you should definitely get a guitar stand. This accessory is also important if you play more than one instrument in performance. Guitar stands are usually made of metal and allow you to stand the guitar upright with the neck pointing upward.

If you use printed music or charts when you practice or perform, you should also consider buying a music stand. If you plan to travel, make sure you consider the portability of the stands you choose. Both guitar and music stands are available in light collapsible models that are easy to transport and store. If you plan to use your stand at home, you may want to get a sturdier model that does not collapse. Both guitar and music stands are available in a wide range of prices. The weight, sturdiness, and portability of these accessories should be considered before making a purchase.

 # Book 2

Music Theory for Guitarists

Your continued study of the mechanics of music will help you to focus on the art of creating it. This book provides a solid introduction to music theory—the study of how musical sounds interrelate melodically, harmonically, and rhythmically. There's also a useful section on tablature and other notation used especially for guitar music.

To learn more about the practical applications of music theory for the guitarist, see "Basic Scale Theory" in *Book 3: Guitar Scale Dictionary* and "Basic Chord Theory" in *Book 4: Guitar Chord Dictionary*.

Rhythm and Metre

Here is a basic guide to understanding how to read rhythm and metre in standard music notation. For further information about reading rhythms for guitar, see "Guitar Tablature and Notation," which shows how rhythm is notated in guitar tablature, chord charts, and lead sheets. To learn more about tempo, see the section, "Structure and Style."

Section Contents

Notes and Rests

As you have learned, the position of the note on the staff indicates a particular *pitch* (that is, how high or low a note sounds). Each note also has a *note value,* or *duration,* (that is, how long the note should last). The duration of a note is counted in *beats.* Here are the basic note shapes and their usual durations. Take the time to memorize the appearance and value of each of these notes.

o A **whole note** lasts for four beats.

♩ A **half note** lasts for two beats.

♩ A **quarter note** lasts for one beat.

♪ An **eighth note** lasts for one-half of a beat.

♪ A **sixteenth note** lasts for one-fourth of a beat.

♪ A **thirty-second note** lasts for one-eighth of a beat.

An eighth note has three components. The circular portion of the note is called the *notehead,* the line is called the *stem,* and the tail is called the *flag.*

♪ ← Flag
  ← Stem
  ← Head

The flag of the sixteenth note is made with two lines, while the thirty-second-note flag is made of three lines. Groups of consecutive eighth, sixteenth, and thirty-second notes are often linked with *beams,* as shown.

Eighth Notes   Sixteenth Notes   Thirty-second Notes

Stem direction is determined by a note's placement on the staff. In either clef, notes occurring below the middle line of the staff have stems that point upward. Notes that occur on or above the middle line should have downward stems. Although this is the preferable rule regarding stem direction, some printed music features notes on the middle line with upward stems. These occur only when other notes in the same measure feature upward stems. Notes connected by a beam should always feature the same stem direction (as determined by the natural stem direction of the majority of notes in the group).

Compare the different notes you have learned and their relative values.

Whole Note:

Half Note:

Quarter Note:

Eighth Note:

Sixteenth Note:

Thirty-second Note:

As you can see, two half-notes equal the duration of one whole-note, four quarter-notes equal the duration of one whole-note, eight eighth-notes equal the duration of one whole-note, and so on.

In order to make it easy to count the rhythm of written music, the staff is divided into sections called *measures*, or *bars*. The vertical lines that divide the staff in this way are called *barlines*. A *double barline* is used to indicate the end of a piece of music. (A lighter double barline is used to divide important sections of a piece.)

Take a look at some of the different note values in measures on the staff. Each measure in this example contains four beats. Count the beats of each measure aloud slowly and evenly while you clap the rhythm indicated by the notes.

Count: <u>1</u>   2   3   4   <u>1</u>   2   <u>3</u>   4   <u>1</u>   <u>2</u>   <u>3</u>   <u>4</u>   <u>1</u> and <u>2</u> and <u>3</u> and <u>4</u> and

The next example combines notes of different durations in each measure. Count the beats aloud as you clap the indicated rhythm. Again, be sure to count slowly and evenly without halting.

Count: <u>1</u>   <u>2</u>   <u>3</u>   4   <u>1</u>   <u>2</u> and <u>3</u>   4   <u>1</u> and <u>2</u> and <u>3</u>   4   <u>1</u> and <u>2</u>   <u>3</u>   4

Reading a Song Melody: Pitch and Rhythm

Now that you are familiar with these basic note values, get ready to combine your knowledge of pitch and rhythm to read a familiar song melody. First count and clap the rhythm of "Jingle Bells," as you did for the previous two exercises. Then play the song on the piano, sing it, or use another instrument to play this melody. Be sure you play it slowly and evenly without halting.

Jingle Bells

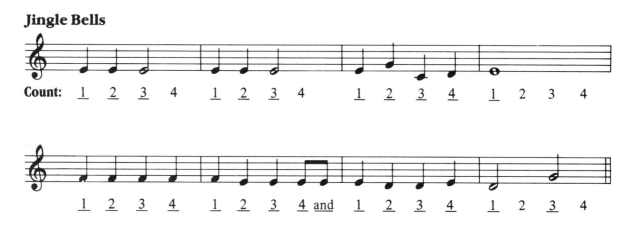

Once you are comfortable playing "Jingle Bells" at a slow speed, try playing it at a medium-fast speed. The technical term for speed in music is *tempo.* Even at this faster tempo, every beat of the song should still be steady and clear.

Rests

Music is usually composed of sounds and silences. The silent beats in music are represented by signs called *rests.* Rests are named and valued in correspondence with the note values you learned in the previous section.

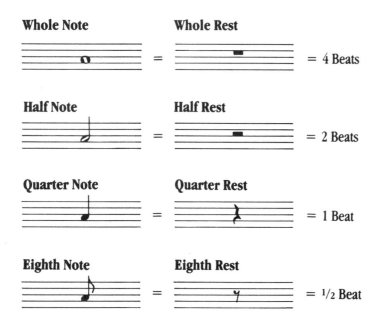

Sixteenth Note   **Sixteenth Rest**

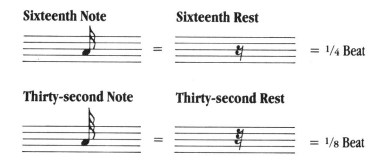

= ¹/₄ Beat

Thirty-second Note   **Thirty-second Rest**

= ¹/₈ Beat

Rests and notes may be combined in the same measure, as long as their combined values add up to the correct number of beats (in this example, four beats to a measure). Count the beats of this phrase as you clap the rhythm of the notes.

Count: 1 2 3 4   1 2 3 4   1 and 2 3 and 4   1 and 2 and 3 and 4 and

Count the beats of this next phrase as you clap the rhythm of the notes. Then play (or sing and play) this melody slowly and evenly.

Count: 1 2 3 4   1 2 3 4   1 2 and 3 and 4 and   1 2 3 4

Pickup Notes

Certain song melodies require an incomplete first measure to provide for a *pickup,* which is simply a note or notes that occur before the first stressed beat of the song. When a musical composition features a partial measure containing a pickup, it usually makes up the remaining beats of the first measure in the last measure of the piece. This means that the last measure of the piece will also be incomplete. You can see how this works in "Polly-Wolly Doodle."

Polly-Wolly Doodle

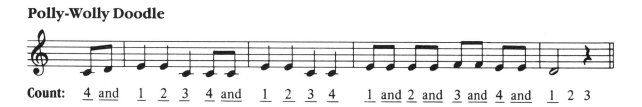

Count: 4 and 1 2 3 4 and 1 2 3 4   1 and 2 and 3 and 4 and 1 2 3

Now let's move on to some more complex note and rest values.

Dotted Notes and Rests

A dot placed after any note or rest means that it should last one-and-a-half times its normal duration. For example, if you add a dot after a half note (which normally lasts two beats), you get a *dotted half note,* which has a duration of three beats.

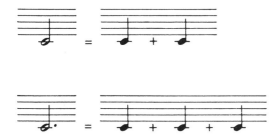

In the same way, if you add a dot to a quarter rest, you get a *dotted quarter rest,* which indicates a silence of one-and-a-half beats.

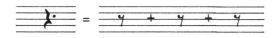

It's easy to understand dotted notes and rests when you compare them with the regular note and rest values you have already learned.

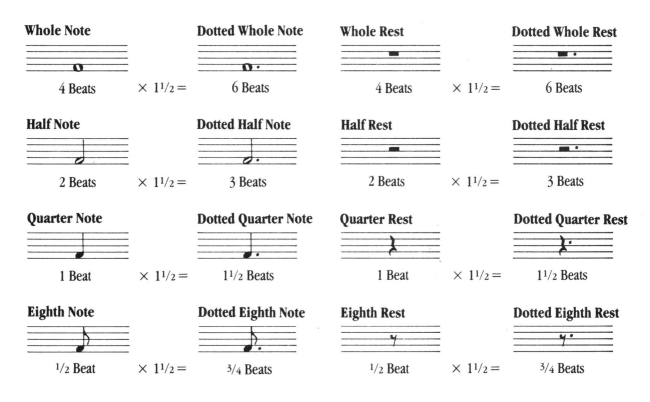

Whole Note		Dotted Whole Note	Whole Rest		Dotted Whole Rest
4 Beats	× 1¹/₂ =	6 Beats	4 Beats	× 1¹/₂ =	6 Beats
Half Note		**Dotted Half Note**	**Half Rest**		**Dotted Half Rest**
2 Beats	× 1¹/₂ =	3 Beats	2 Beats	× 1¹/₂ =	3 Beats
Quarter Note		**Dotted Quarter Note**	**Quarter Rest**		**Dotted Quarter Rest**
1 Beat	× 1¹/₂ =	1¹/₂ Beats	1 Beat	× 1¹/₂ =	1¹/₂ Beats
Eighth Note		**Dotted Eighth Note**	**Eighth Rest**		**Dotted Eighth Rest**
¹/₂ Beat	× 1¹/₂ =	³/₄ Beats	¹/₂ Beat	× 1¹/₂ =	³/₄ Beats

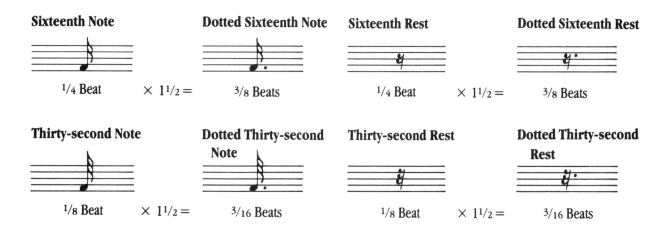

Sixteenth Note	Dotted Sixteenth Note	Sixteenth Rest	Dotted Sixteenth Rest
¹/₄ Beat × 1¹/₂ =	³/₈ Beats	¹/₄ Beat × 1¹/₂ =	³/₈ Beats

Thirty-second Note	Dotted Thirty-second Note	Thirty-second Rest	Dotted Thirty-second Rest
¹/₈ Beat × 1¹/₂ =	³/₁₆ Beats	¹/₈ Beat × 1¹/₂ =	³/₁₆ Beats

Take the time to memorize the appearance and value of each dotted note and rest. Then count the beats in the next example as you clap the rhythm indicated by the notes. (Notice how the dotted eighth notes are connected by beams to the sixteenth notes in the third measure.)

Count: 1 2 3 4   1 and 2 and 3 and 4 and   1 2 3 4 2 2 3 4 3 2 3 4 4 2 3 4   1 2 3 4

Now combine your knowledge of pitch and rhythm as you play (or play and sing) the opening phrase of "I've Been Working on the Railroad."

I've Been Working on the Railroad

You may also encounter a *double dotted note* in written music. Two dots indicate that the note is worth one and three-fourths of its normal value. In this way, a double dotted whole note lasts for seven beats. A double dotted half note lasts for three-and-a-half beats.

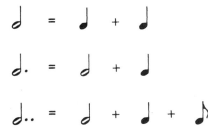

By now, you are quite familiar with basic note and rest values. Let's look at some new note values and signs that express information about the rhythm of a piece of music.

Ties

Some notes are actually made up of two note values which are linked together with a *tie*. A tie indicates that a note be held for the combined length of the two tied notes. For this reason, the two notes that are tied together on the staff always have exactly the same pitch. Ties are often used to link two notes across the barline, as can be seen in the last two bars of this excerpt from "Daisy Bell (A Bicycle Built for Two)."

Daisy Bell (A Bicycle Built for Two)

Sometimes tied notes are used within a bar to make the rhythm easy to count within a certain musical context.

Ties may also be used in sequence for this purpose.

If a note altered by an accidental is tied across the barline, the second note is also affected. Any subsequent notes of the same pitch will be unaffected.

Because of their similar appearance, ties are often confused with *slurs*, which are defined in the later section on accents and articulation. The way to tell them apart is to remember that ties link notes of the same pitch, while slurs always link notes of different pitches.

Extended Rests

Extended rests are used primarily in orchestral or band music since these genres often require that certain instruments rest for several bars. A numeral above the sign indicates the number of measures for which the instruments should rest. This sign indicates that the rest should last for twelve bars.

Pauses

Sometimes a composer or arranger wishes to indicate that the regular beat or tempo of a piece should hold or pause for a moment on a specific note or rest. This hold or pause is indicated with a *fermata,* as shown in the following two phrases of "For He's a Jolly Good Fellow." (The amount of time which the indicated note or rest should be held is left to the discretion of the performer.)

For He's a Jolly Good Fellow

For   he's   a jol - ly good   fel - low; Which   no- bod- y   can   de - ny.

Another kind of pause of indefinite length is indicated with two slashes above the staff (//). This marking is called a *cesura* (or *caesura*)—and indicates that the note is held for its normal time value and then followed by an abrupt pause at the performer's discretion.

Triplets and Other Note Groupings

Composers and arrangers sometimes need to divide a basic note value into three notes of equal value. These three notes are collectively called a *triplet,* which is indicated by the numeral *3* on the beam.

The "eighth-notes" in the triplet above are each worth one-third of one beat. Try clapping the rhythm of "March of the Wooden Soldiers"—and then play it on the piano, or use the instrument of your choice to play this example.

March of the Wooden Soldiers (from *The Nutcracker*)

1   2 and a   3   4   1   2   3   4   1   2 and a   3   4   1   2   3   4

Other note values may be used in a triplet. Here's an example of "quarter notes" linked in a triplet. Notice that a bracket is used when notes cannot be joined by a beam. Each of these is worth one-third of the value of a half note, or two-thirds of a beat. Play the first phrase of "Hey There, You With the Stars in Your Eyes."

Hey There, You With the Stars in Your Eyes

Triplets can also contain dotted notes and rests. Thus, in "Lilliburlero," the dotted "eighth notes" in each triplet are actually worth one-half of a beat. Each "sixteenth note" is worth one-sixth of a beat.

Lilliburlero

You may also encounter sixteenth-note triplets or thirty-second-note triplets, as shown in this example.

Duplets do not commonly occur in popular music. They are used in music written in compound time signatures to indicate that two notes receive the value commonly afforded to three notes in that timing.

The duplets in this phrase in $\frac{6}{8}$ indicate that the groups of two eighth-notes are played in the time usually allotted to three eighth notes. This means that each note of the duplet is worth one and a half beats in this time signature.

Quadruplets, quintuplets, and *sextuplets* are also infrequent.

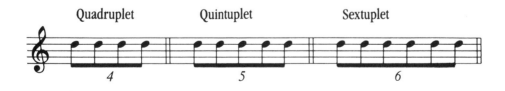

Simple Time Signatures

Every musical composition has a *time signature* at the beginning of the first staff. This symbol indicates two important facts about the overall rhythm of the piece.

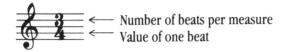

    ←— Number of beats per measure
    ←— Value of one beat

The top number of the time signature indicates how many beats there are in each measure. The bottom number determines which type of note is worth one beat.

2 = Half Note
4 = Quarter Note
8 = Eighth Note

The time signature is a guidepost to the overall rhythm of a piece of music. Each time signature has a characteristic pattern of stressed and unstressed beats. A composer or arranger chooses the time signature which best matches the natural stresses of a particular piece or section of music.

In the sections that follow, you'll take a look at some basic time signatures and their characteristic patterns of stress.

$\frac{4}{4}$ Time

$\frac{4}{4}$ (pronounced "four-four") is the most common time signature used in written music. Much of the music we've examined in the book so far has been in $\frac{4}{4}$ time—that is, with four beats in each measure and the quarter note lasting for its natural value of one beat.

    ←— 4 beats per measure
    ←— A quarter note gets one beat

The $\frac{4}{4}$ time signature is so prevalent that it is sometimes referred to as "common time" and notated with this shorthand symbol.

Each time signature has a natural, characteristic pattern of stressed and unstressed beats. The first beat of each measure in any time signature receives the most stress. In $\frac{4}{4}$ time, the third beat is also stressed, but to a lesser extent.

Stress   Stress

"Jingle Bells" provides a strong example of the natural stresses which occur in $\frac{4}{4}$ time. (The stressed beats are indicated with boldface numbers.)

Jingle Bells

1   2   3   4   1   2   3   4   1   2   3   4   1   2   3   4

$\frac{3}{4}$ Time

$\frac{3}{4}$ (or "three-four") time is also sometimes called *waltz time,* since this is the characteristic time signature of this dance form. However, there are many other types of compositions that employ this time signature. In $\frac{3}{4}$ time, the quarter note still receives its normal value, but there are only three beats in every measure.

   ⟵ 3 beats per measure
   ⟵ A quarter note gets one beat

The natural stress of $\frac{3}{4}$ time falls on the first beat of each measure only. Sing or hum the first phrase of "Drink to Me Only With Thine Eyes" to get a feeling for the natural, lilting stress of $\frac{3}{4}$ time.

Drink to Me Only With Thine Eyes

1   2   3   1   2   3   1   2   3   1   2   3

1   2   3   1   2   3   1   2   3

$\frac{2}{4}$ Time

$\frac{2}{4}$ time calls for only two beats in each measure with a stress on every other beat. Richard Wagner's familiar "Wedding March" illustrates the strong and regular stress pattern of this time signature. Notice the bass clef.

Wedding March

$\frac{2}{2}$ Time

So far, we've looked at time signatures that call for the quarter note to receive its natural value of one beat. $\frac{2}{2}$ time, or *cut time,* indicates that a half note lasts for only one beat—with two beats in each measure. $\frac{2}{2}$ time is usually noted with this shorthand symbol (¢). This time signature makes it easier for musicians to read music with many short note values or complex rhythms. Here's the traditional fiddle tune "Turkey in the Straw" in $\frac{2}{2}$ time. Notice that the stresses fall on every other beat.

Turkey in the Straw

Take a look at how much more difficult this song is to read when notated in $\frac{2}{4}$ time. The sixteenth notes seem harder to count at a glance than the eighth notes in the above example.

Turkey in the Straw

$\frac{3}{2}$ and $\frac{4}{2}$ Time

$\frac{3}{2}$ and $\frac{4}{2}$ time signatures also call for the half note to equal one beat.

$\frac{2}{8}$, $\frac{3}{8}$, and $\frac{4}{8}$ Time

Some time signatures call for an eighth note to be valued as one beat. Try counting aloud as you clap the rhythm of these phrases. (Stressed beats are indicated with boldface numbers.)

All of the time signatures we've looked at so far are called *simple time signatures* because they require a basic arrangement of the number of beats in each measure and the value of each beat.

Compound Time Signatures

You are already familiar with the simple time signatures, like $\frac{3}{4}$ and $\frac{4}{4}$. *Compound time signatures* obey the same rules as simple time signatures, but the rhythmic stresses they create in music are based upon beats that are always counted in multiples of three. The top number of a compound time signature is always a multiple of three to reflect this pattern of stress. Let's look at the most common compound time signature to appear in written music, $\frac{6}{8}$.

6 beats per measure
An eighth note gets one beat

As you can see, there are six beats to the measure, with an eighth note valued at one beat. Notice that a stressed beat occurs every three eighth-note beats, providing two stresses in every measure. This is illustrated by boldface numbers in the first phrase of "The Irish Washerwoman."

The Irish Washerwoman

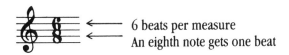

1 2 3 4 5 6   1 2 3 4 5 6   1 2 3 4 5 6   1 2 3 4 5 6

This same counting pattern occurs in music written in $\frac{6}{4}$ and $\frac{6}{16}$.

1 2 3 4 5 6   1 2 3 4 5 6   1 2 3 4 5 6   1 2 3 4 5 6

Time signatures which call for nine beats in a measure also create a stress every three beats. In $\frac{9}{8}$ time, there are three stresses in every measure.

1   2   3   4   5   6   7   8   9   1   2   3   4   5   6   7   8   9

$\frac{12}{8}$ time features twelve beats—and so four stresses—in every measure.

1 2 3 4 5 6 7 8 9 10 11 12   1 2 3 4 5 6 7 8 9 10 11 12

As with their "simple" counterparts, $\frac{3}{4}$ and $\frac{4}{4}$ time, the first stress in each measure of $\frac{9}{8}$ and $\frac{12}{8}$ time is generally the strongest. You may sometimes encounter *complex time signatures*—like $\frac{5}{4}$, $\frac{5}{8}$, $\frac{7}{4}$, or $\frac{7}{8}$—which call for unusual numbers of beats in each measure. These time signatures support different patterns of stress. $\frac{5}{4}$ and $\frac{7}{8}$ time are each illustrated below in a typical pattern of stress.

You may find that a time signature changes in the middle of a piece to create an entirely new rhythm. This can be seen in the traditional carol, "Here We Come A-Wassailing." At the beginning of the song's chorus, the timing changes from $\frac{6}{8}$ to $\frac{4}{4}$.

Here We Come A-Wassailing

With a little practice, you should be able to count any new timing correctly. To familiarize yourself with the more commonly used compound time signatures, practice counting and playing these melody phrases.

Sweet Betsy From Pike

Boogie Woogie Bugle Boy

Barcarolle (from *Tales of Hoffman*)

Beautiful Dreamer

Keys and Intervals

The way pitches are organized in a piece of music determines the key. The distance from one pitch to another is called an interval. These are the building blocks of all melody and harmony. This section provides an overview of the important aspects of musical pitch.

To learn more about the practical applications of this information for the guitarist, see "Basic Scale Theory" in *Book 3: Guitar Scale Dictionary* and "Basic Chord Theory" in *Book 4: Guitar Chord Dictionary*.

Section Contents

Accidentals

Until this point in your study of written music, all of the musical examples provided have contained no sharps or flats. You have become quite familiar with those notes represented by the white keys of the piano: A, B, C, D, E, F, and G. As you may have already noticed, the black keys of the piano keyboard provide pitches in between these notes. These pitches are collectively called *accidentals*. They are more commonly called *sharp* or *flat notes,* depending on their musical context. The names of these notes are formed by adding a *sharp sign* (♯) or *flat sign* (♭) after the note letter name. These signs, as well as the notes themselves, are often simply called *sharps* and *flats*.

Sharps

Let's take a look at the sharp notes as they relate to a portion of the piano keyboard.

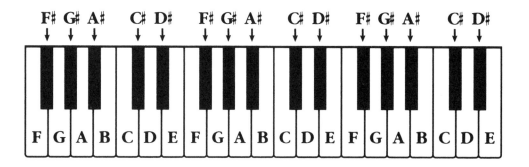

As you can see, each sharp key occurs just above the white key with the same letter name. Thus, the black note in between the C and D notes is labeled *C♯*, the black note in between the D and E keys is *D♯*, and so on. Notice that no sharp occurs between the E and F keys, or between the B and C keys. Here's the complete sequence of natural and sharp note names.

A - A♯ - B - C - C♯ - D - D♯ - E - F - F♯ - G - G♯ - A

The distance between each of these notes is called a *half step.* A sequence of half steps is called a *chromatic scale.* Let's take a look at the chromatic scale, beginning on Middle C, as notated on the staff in treble clef.

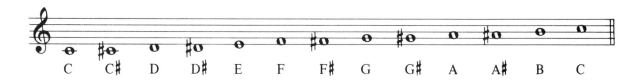

Here's the same scale in bass clef, an octave lower.

C   C♯   D   D♯   E   F   F♯   G   G♯   A   A♯   B   C

Try playing these scales on the piano, or on the instrument of your choice. If you play an instrument other than the piano, refer to a note fingering chart to find out how to play each of these new notes. If you are a singer, practice singing the chromatic scale as you play along on the piano or guitar. Take the time to memorize the position and name of each of the sharp notes as they appear on the keyboard and staff.

Flats

Sometimes the black keys of the piano are viewed as *flat notes* rather than sharp notes. The reason for having two names for each of these notes will be clear when we discuss *key signatures* in the next section. For now, let's get to know the names of the flat notes and then compare them to those of the sharp notes.

A flat note occurs one note lower than the white key of the same letter name on the piano keyboard. The flat sign appears after the letter name of the lowered white key to indicate the black-key name. Thus, the black-key note in between the C and D notes is labeled *D♭*, the black-key note in between the D and E keys is *E♭,* and so on. No flat occurs between the E and F keys, or between the B and C keys.

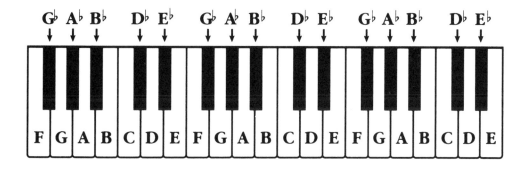

Here's the complete sequence of natural and flat note names.

A - B♭ - B - C - D♭ - D - E♭ - E - F - G♭ - G - A♭ - A

Let's take a look at how the chromatic scale is notated using flats in treble clef.

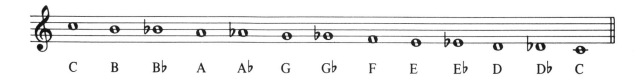

C   B   B♭   A   A♭   G   G♭   F   E   E♭   D   D♭   C

Here's the same scale in bass clef, an octave lower.

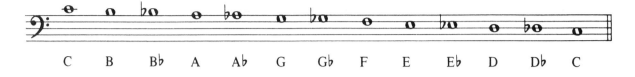

C   B   Bb   A   Ab   G   Gb   F   E   Eb   D   Db   C

Take the time to memorize the name and position of each of these flat notes as they appear on the keyboard and staff. Now play these scales on the piano—or play the appropriate scale on the treble or bass instrument of your choice.

Here's an important rule which applies to both sharps and flats: If a note appears with a sharp or flat sign, all subsequent notes in the same position on the staff of that measure are also affected by that sign.

As you can see in the two preceding examples, the barline cancels both sharp and flat signs.

Naturals

A *natural sign* also cancels a sharp or flat sign that has appeared with a note of the same position. Because a barline cancels all flat and sharp signs, there's no need to use a natural sign unless you wish to cancel a flat or sharp that has already occurred in the same measure. Once a natural sign has been used, all other subsequent notes in the same position on the staff in that measure are affected by the natural sign.

As you might expect, a natural sign may be cancelled by a flat or sharp sign with a note of the same position in the same measure. (Notice that the barline then cancels the sharp.)

Some pieces contain both sharps and flats. Whether a note is flatted or sharped depends on its particular musical function in the piece. But, as a general rule, an accidental that leads up to a natural note is written as a sharp note—and an accidental that leads down to a natural note is written as a flat note. This rule is illustrated in "Melancholy Baby."

Melancholy Baby

Double Sharps and Flats

Though they rarely occur, you may come across a *double sharp* or *double flat* in written music. These accidentals are seldom necessary—and keys that may require their use are generally avoided. However, double sharps or double flats are sometimes used to maintain a logical pattern of notes on the staff.

A *double sharp* (×) raises the indicated note by two half-steps. If the note is already sharped in the key signature, or by a previous accidental in the same measure, the double sharp raises the pitch by one half-step only. In other words, a double sharp raises any note two half-steps from its natural position. Thus, F× is another name for the G note. An F× note is used in the following example to preserve the visual pattern of ascending thirds in the key of E major.

If a G note were used instead of F× in this passage, the pattern of thirds would be violated, and thus more difficult to read.

Sometimes a *natural sharp* sign is used to return a double sharp note to a sharped note in the same measure. However, most authorities agree that the natural sign is superfluous, and a sharp sign alone will suffice, as shown at right.

You may also sometimes see a *double natural* employed to cancel a double sharp completely in the same measure. However, a single natural is quite sufficient for this purpose, as shown at right.

A *double flat* sign lowers the indicated note by two half steps. Here, B♭♭ is used to preserve the pattern of descending thirds in the key of E♭ major.

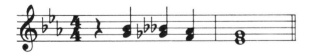

A *natural flat* sign or *double natural* may occur in some printed music, but the single flat or natural sign is preferable for the partial or complete cancellation of a double flat, as shown at right.

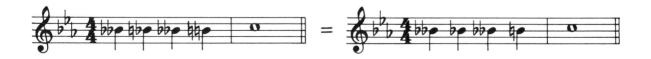

Major Key Signatures

So far, we've looked at sharp, flat, and natural notes that are individually added to written music. These notes are called *accidentals* or *altered notes*. Many pieces of music require that certain notes be sharped or flatted as a general rule. The number of sharps or flats which occur regularly in a piece of music determines the *key*. Rather than writing in a sharp or flat sign every time one should occur, these signs are written in a *key signature* at the beginning of each staff.

Composers and arrangers place music in different keys to accommodate the needs of the particular ranges of the voices or instruments for which they are writing. Certain keys are easier to play on certain instruments. Using different keys for the individual sections or songs in a larger work—such as a symphony or a Broadway show—adds variety to a performance. This is important to remember if you are planning your own concert, or writing music for others to perform.

The Key of C Major

Most of the musical examples in the book so far have been written in the *key of C major*, which has no sharps or flats. Thus, all the notes of the C major scale occur on the white keys of the piano keyboard. Once you understand the construction of the scale in the key of C major, you'll be able to build the scale and key signature for every other major key.

As you already know, the shortest distance between two notes is called a half step. A *whole step* is the equivalent of two half steps. Let's examine the pattern of whole steps and half steps in the C major scale.

C Major Scale

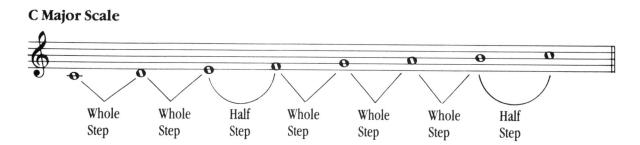

Take the time to memorize this important pattern, because it is the blueprint for all other major scales: whole step, whole step, half step, whole step, whole step, whole step, half step. If you play an instrument other than the piano, take the time to learn the fingering and sound of the notes of the C major scale on your instrument. Singers should sing this scale with piano or guitar accompaniment.

The Sharp Keys

Once you are quite familiar with the step-by-step pattern of the C major scale, take a look at the *G major scale*. The notes of this scale are the building blocks for music in the *key of G major*. Notice that this scale requires an F♯ note in order to follow the proper step-by-step pattern for major scales.

G Major Scale

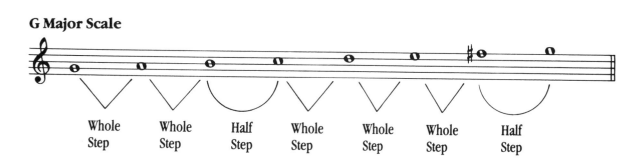

Whole Step   Whole Step   Half Step   Whole Step   Whole Step   Whole Step   Half Step

Since the F♯ note is a regular feature in the key of G major, it is represented in the key signature after the clef on every staff of the piece. This means that all notes which occur in the F position in the piece (unless otherwise marked) will be sharped—as in this excerpt from Schubert's "Unfinished Symphony."

Theme From the Unfinished Symphony

Keep in mind that the F♯ note indicated in the preceding key signature applies to all F♯ note positions in the piece, no matter how high or low. This applies to the bass clef as well.

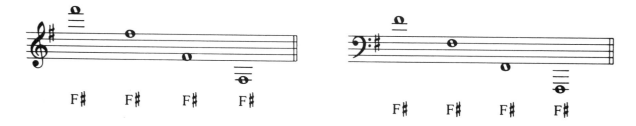

F♯   F♯   F♯   F♯   F♯   F♯   F♯   F♯

The *D major scale* follows the same step-by-step pattern as the C and G major scales.

D Major Scale

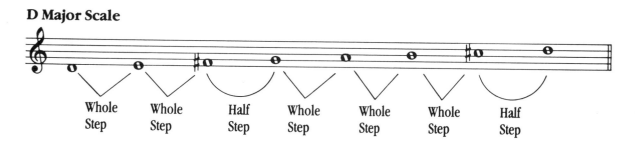

Whole Step   Whole Step   Half Step   Whole Step   Whole Step   Whole Step   Half Step

As you can see, this scale features two sharps. Its key signature is notated on the treble and bass staves as follows.

Let's take a look at all of the major key signatures and corresponding scales that contain sharps. Although it is not necessary to include any sharp signs next to the notes of these scales, they are shown here in parentheses for your reference.

The Sharp Keys

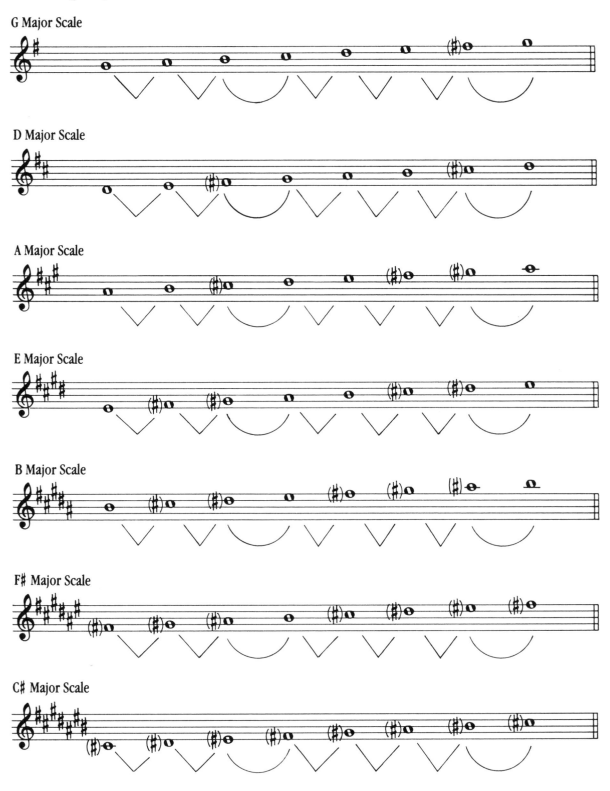

G Major Scale

D Major Scale

A Major Scale

E Major Scale

B Major Scale

F# Major Scale

C# Major Scale

Here's a trick for identifying the major key represented by any key signature that contains sharps. Find the line or space position that is one half-step higher than the position of the last sharp to the right in the key signature. This position names the major key. As you can see, this pattern is similar in both clefs.

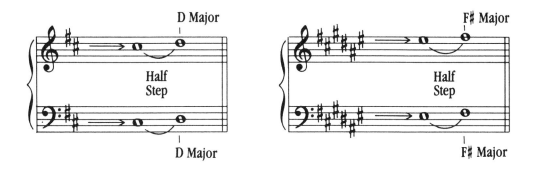

The easiest way to memorize the order of the sharps as they appear in the key signatures is to examine the pattern of sharps in the key of C♯ major, which features all seven sharps.

Take a look at the distance between each consecutive sharp in the key signature of C♯ major. Stepping down the staff by lines and spaces, the second sharp (C♯) is three note positions lower on the staff than the first sharp (F♯). The third sharp (G♯) is four positions higher on the staff than the second sharp (C♯)— and the fourth sharp is three steps lower than the third.

In order to avoid placing the fifth sharp of the pattern (A♯) on a leger line above the staff, this note is moved down an octave to the A♯ which occurs in the second space of the staff. The last two sharps (E♯ and B♯) return to the original pattern.

This pattern is identical in bass clef.

The Flat Keys

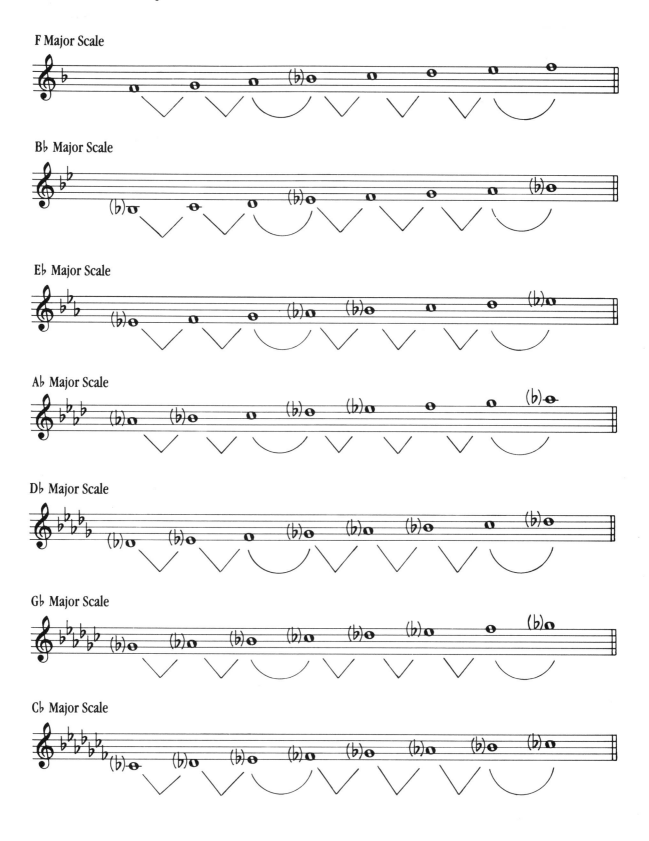

Here's a trick for identifying the major key represented by a key signature with flats. Find the second to the last flat of the key signature. Add a flat to the letter name of that note position and you've got the name of the key. (You'll need to memorize the fact that one flat indicates the key of F major.)

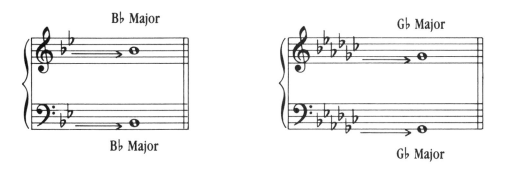

To understand the pattern of flats, take a look at the distance between each consecutive flat in the key signature of C♭ major. Stepping up the staff by lines and spaces, the second flat (E♭) is three note positions higher on the staff than the first flat (B♭). The third flat (A♭) is four positions lower on the staff than the second flat (E♭)—the fourth flat is three steps higher than the third, and so on.

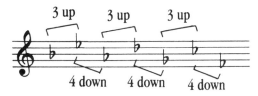

This pattern is the same in bass clef.

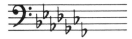

Minor Key Signatures

As you know, music may be written in different keys to accommodate the ranges of particular voices or instruments. Another reason for writing a piece in a particular key is to lend a special tonal color, or *tonality*, to a piece. Many of the musical excerpts you have studied in this book so far have been written in a major key, and therefore have major tonalities. Sometimes a composer chooses to use a *minor key* to lend an introspective or sad quality to a piece. This section explores the different minor keys and how they are formed.

There are three forms of the minor scale: the *natural minor,* the *melodic minor,* and the *harmonic minor.* Let's compare the familiar C major scale with these three minor forms. Since all C minor scales use the same starting note as the key of C major, each are called the *tonic minor* of this major key. For this same reason, C major and C minor are also sometimes called *parallel keys.*

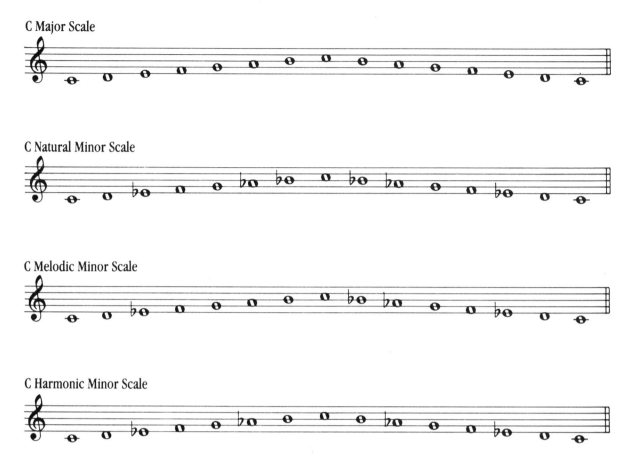

Notice that the third, sixth, and seventh notes (or *degrees*) of the natural minor scale are lowered by one half-step. The melodic minor features a lowered third on the way up the scale, and a lowered third, sixth, and seventh on the way down. The third and sixth of the harmonic minor scale are lowered by one half-step, whether ascending or descending.

In order to avoid the routine writing of the accidentals necessary to create these minor forms, music written in the key of C minor features a key signature with three flats (like the key of E♭ major). This brings the need for accidentals to a minimum. In this key signature, an accidental is required only on the sixth and seventh degrees of the ascending C melodic minor scale—and on the seventh degree of the C harmonic minor scale.

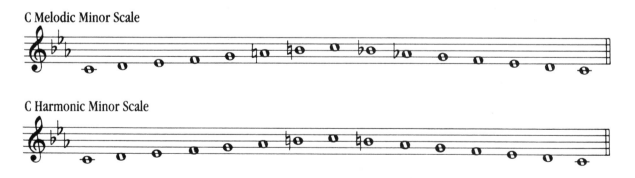

Because the key of C minor uses the same key signature as E♭ major, it is known as the *relative minor* of this major key. Correspondingly, the key of E♭ major is known as the *relative major* of C minor. Presented below are all the harmonic and melodic scale forms in every minor key. The name of each relative major key is shown in parentheses. Notice that the relative major key is always three half-steps (a minor third) up from the note named by the corresponding minor key. Take the time to practice playing or singing each of these minor scales until they become quite familiar.

Key of A Minor (Relative Minor of C Major)

A Melodic Minor Scale

A Harmonic Minor Scale

Key of E Minor (Relative Minor of G Major)

E Melodic Minor Scale

E Harmonic Minor Scale

Key of B Minor (Relative Minor of D Major)

B Melodic Minor Scale

B Harmonic Minor Scale

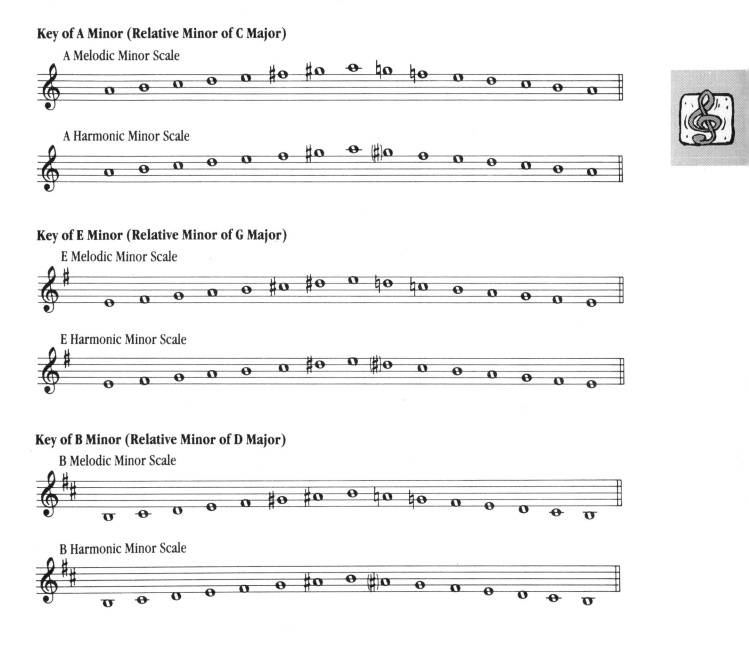

Key of F♯ Minor (Relative Minor of A Major)

F♯ Melodic Minor Scale

F♯ Harmonic Minor Scale

Key of C♯ Minor (Relative Minor of E Major)

C♯ Melodic Minor Scale

C♯ Harmonic Minor Scale

Key of G♯ Minor (Relative Minor of B Major)

G♯ Melodic Minor Scale

G♯ Harmonic Minor Scale

Key of D♯ Minor (Relative Minor of F♯ Major)

D♯ Melodic Minor Scale

D♯ Harmonic Minor Scale

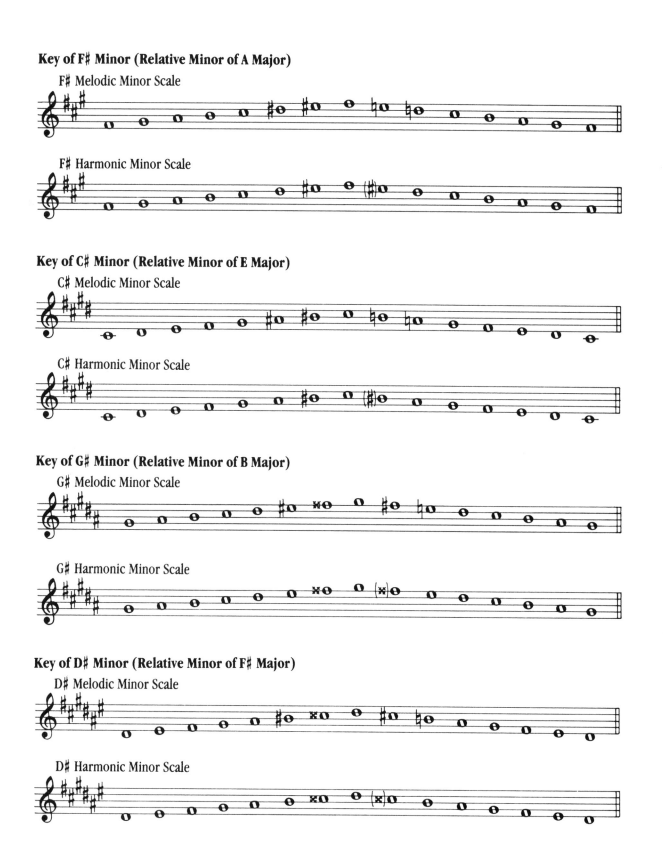

Key of A♯ Minor (Relative Minor of C♯ Major)

A♯ Melodic Minor Scale

A♯ Harmonic Minor Scale

Key of D Minor (Relative Minor of F Major)

D Melodic Minor Scale

D Harmonic Minor Scale

Key of G Minor (Relative Minor of B♭ Major)

G Melodic Minor Scale

G Harmonic Minor Scale

Key of C Minor (Relative Minor of E♭ Major)

C Melodic Minor Scale

C Harmonic Minor Scale

Key of F Minor (Relative Minor of A♭ Major)

F Melodic Minor Scale

F Harmonic Minor Scale

Key of B♭ Minor (Relative Minor of D♭ Major)

B♭ Melodic Minor Scale

B♭ Harmonic Minor Scale

Key of E♭ Minor (Relative Minor of G♭ Major)

E♭ Melodic Minor Scale

E♭ Harmonic Minor Scale

Key of A♭ Minor (Relative Minor of C♭ Major)

A♭ Melodic Minor Scale

A♭ Harmonic Minor Scale

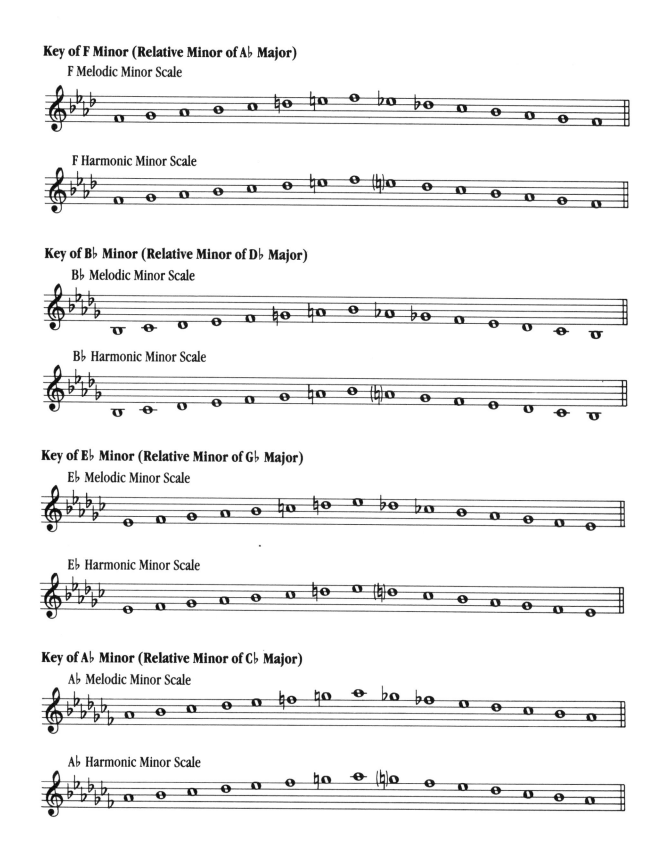

Intervals

The distance between two notes is called an *interval*. To understand how intervals are named, let's look at the *degrees* (or numerical names) of the notes of the C major scale.

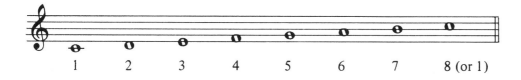

Diatonic Intervals

Here are the intervals which correspond to the scale in C major. These are called *diatonic intervals*. Practice playing or singing these intervals until you are familiar with the name and characteristic sound of each one.

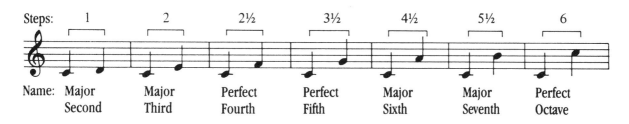

Some intervals move from a low note to a higher note, while others move from high to low. All of these are called *melodic intervals*. Now try playing the notes of each interval backward—that is, from the highest to lowest note.

When the notes of these intervals are played simultaneously, they are called *harmonic intervals*. Listen to the notes of each interval played simultaneously on the piano or guitar.

Intervals may occur on different notes of the scale in different keys. It's easy to identify an interval by its position on the staff. For example:

 An interval of a second always contains one note on a line and one note on an adjacent space.

 An interval of a third always either contains two notes on adjacent lines or two notes on adjacent spaces.

 A fourth always contains a note on a space and a note on a line with one line and one space in between.

 A fifth always contains two notes on spaces with one space skipped, or two notes on lines with one line skipped.

 A sixth always contains one note on a line and one note on a space with two lines and two spaces skipped.

 A seventh always contains two notes on spaces with two spaces skipped, or two notes on lines with two lines skipped.

 An octave always contains one note on a line and one note on a space, with three lines and three spaces skipped.

Chromatic Intervals

When a diatonic interval is made larger or smaller by an interval of a half step, a *chromatic interval* results. Let's take a look at the now familiar diatonic intervals and their corresponding lowered and raised chromatic intervals in sequence.

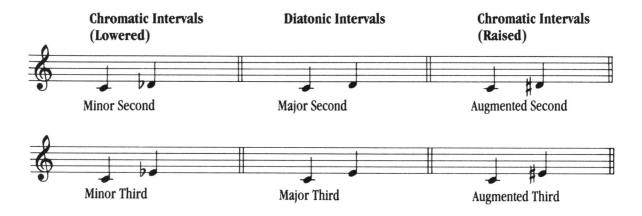

Chromatic Intervals (Lowered)	Diatonic Intervals	Chromatic Intervals (Raised)
Minor Second	Major Second	Augmented Second
Minor Third	Major Third	Augmented Third

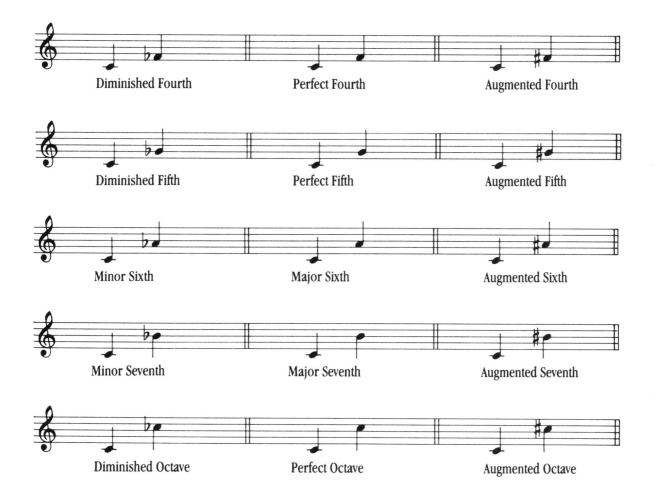

One interval that has not been featured in the preceding charts is the *perfect unison.* The perfect unison may be diminished and augmented like any other perfect interval.

Take the time to memorize the name and appearance of each of the chromatic intervals. Play (or sing and play) each interval backward and forward until you are familiar with its sound. You'll find that certain intervals—like the augmented second and minor third—sound exactly alike. Determine which other intervals sound alike. (These intervals occur in a predictable pattern.)

When naming a chromatic interval, first determine the name of its unaltered form (second, third, fourth, and so on). Then determine the chromatic interval's name by ascertaining whether the diatonic interval has been made larger or smaller by one half-step (according to the major scale of the lower note). Label each of these diatonic and chromatic intervals. Be sure to consider the clef and key signature of each.

Many teachers recommend that you memorize musical intervals by association with their occurrence in famous melodies. Here are some suggested melody phrases to use for this purpose. The indicated interval is shown in brackets. (Notice that the interval of a major seventh, as illustrated in "Bali Hai," is formed between the first and third notes. The perfect fifth occurs between the second and third notes of "Twinkle, Twinkle, Little Star.") The common abbreviation for each interval is also included above the bracket. It's a good idea to commit these abbreviations to memory as well. You should feel free to come up with other melody phrases to use when memorizing these intervals.

Give yourself some more practice at identifying intervals by examining other music and labelling each interval of the melody. The study and practice of intervals is an important listening skill. The mastery of this skill is central to a musician's ability to sightread written music. You may find it useful and fun to get together with a friend for cooperative study of this subject—and take turns playing, singing, and identifying intervals together.

Structure and Style

Written music often includes directions regarding its structure and interpretation. These markings help the composer or arranger to communicate with the player. Some of them are mere shorthand ways to convey repeated notes or sections, while others have more to do with the speed of the piece or the manner in which the music is to be performed. This section provides an overview of common stylistic and structural markings.

Section Contents

Repeats and Endings

In basic terms, an instrumental piece or song should have a clear beginning which leads to the body of the piece (often called the *development section*) and an effective ending. Popular songs often feature an *introduction* or *verse section* as an opener—leading to the *chorus* or main section of the piece. In classical music, there are many different conventions for arranging the individual sections of a work.

Let's take a look at the different markings and symbols that guide the musician through the various sections of a musical composition. Bear in mind that the musical examples used in this section are thumbnail illustrations of the functions of these markings and symbols. In a full-sized musical composition, several pages of music may actually occur between symbols—so it's a good idea to review their placement and meaning before you begin to play or sing a particular piece.

Repeat Sign

Most styles of music call for their individual sections to be repeated at times. In fact, this kind of repetition is often important to the structure of a musical composition. Two dots before a double bar form a *repeat sign*. If this sign occurs at the end of the piece, it indicates that you should repeat the entire piece once from the beginning. Play "Hot Cross Buns" twice through in tempo.

If a repeat sign occurs in the middle of a piece, go back to the beginning and repeat the section before going on.

If a mirror image of the repeat sign occurs earlier in the piece, the performer should only repeat from that point onward. This version of "Hot Cross Buns" has a pickup measure at the beginning. The inverted repeat sign indicates that you should skip this measure when you repeat the piece.

Repeat Markings: Da Capo and Dal Segno

D.C. is an abbreviation of the Italian phrase *Da Capo* (pronounced "dah cahpo"), meaning "from the head." This marking means the same thing as a single repeat sign—repeat the piece from its beginning.

D.S. is short for the Italian phrase *Dal Segno* (pronounced "dahl senyo"), meaning "from the sign." *D.S.* means that the performer should go back to the *dal segno sign* (𝄋) and repeat the section.

Alternate Endings

Sometimes a composer or arranger wants a section repeated with an alternate ending. A bracket and numeral is used in these instances to mark the measure or measures of each different ending. This means that you should skip the *first ending* on the repeat and go on to the *second ending*.

Let's look at how the markings, *Da Capo* and *Dal Segno* may be used to indicate alternate endings. *D.C. al Coda* tells you to repeat the piece until you reach the *coda sign* (⊕)—then skip to the next coda sign, and play or sing the *coda,* which is a short ending section (literally "tail" in Italian).

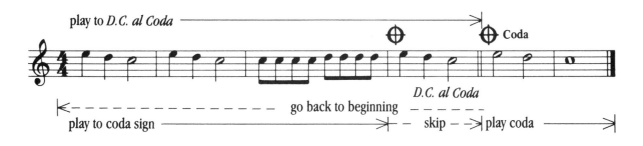

D.S. al Coda indicates that you should repeat from the *dal segno* sign. Once you reach the coda sign, skip to the next coda sign, and play or sing the coda section. *D.C. al Coda* and *D.S. al Coda* are sometimes written *D.C. al* ⊕ and *D.S. al* ⊕

Fine (pronounced "feenay") is the Italian word for "end." This marking is used in conjunction with repeat markings to indicate the point at which the piece ends. *D.C. al Fine* indicates that you should go back to the beginning of the piece and repeat until you come to the marking *Fine*.

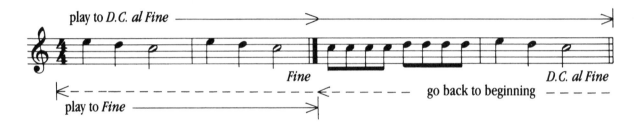

D.S. al Fine tells you to go back to the *dal segno* sign and repeat until the point marked *Fine*.

Articulations and Ornaments

Different accents and articulations are used to create distinctive phrases or points of interest in a piece.

Staccato

If a dot appears above or below a note, that note should be played or sung with a short and crisp action called *staccato*. Staccato notes with upward stems feature the staccato marking beneath the notehead. Notes with downward stems feature the dot above the notehead. In order to create a short, sharp sound, a staccato note receives less than half its indicated value. For example, quarter notes with this marking will be approximately equivalent to sixteenth notes.

A triangle above or below a note also indicates that it should be treated as a staccato, though this marking generally calls for somewhat more stress.

Accents

Notes marked with any of these *accent signs* are to be played or sung with a strong accent and held for their full note value.

The symbols *sf*, *sz*, and *sfz* (short for *sforzando*), as well as *rf* (short for *rinforzando*), indicate that a very strong accent be applied to the designated note.

Slur

A curved line connecting two or more notes calls for them to be played smoothly. The *slur* should not be confused with the *tie*, which calls for two notes of the same pitch to be played as one note value.

Sometimes a slur is used with staccato markings to indicate that the notes be played halfway between staccato and legato—that is, they are still detached, yet somewhat smooth.

Phrase Mark

A *phrase mark* is a curved line used by composers and arrangers to indicate the natural punctuation of a musical piece. Phrase marks are usually used to highlight longer passages than slurs, as shown in the first two phrases of "Joy to the World." Notice that a tie also appears in the last measure of this example.

Joy to the World

When used in a song, phrase marks often correspond with the natural punctuation of its lyrics. This type of agreement of phrasing between melody and lyrics helps make a song memorable and structurally sound.

Grace Note

The *grace note* is a small note that adjoins a full-sized note. It is usually depicted as a small eighth note with a slash through its flag and stem. The grace note you will encounter most often in written music is the *unaccented grace note*. This note should be played as quickly as possible just before the natural beat of the note that follows. Here is the grace note, both as it is notated and as it is actually played.

Unaccented Grace Note

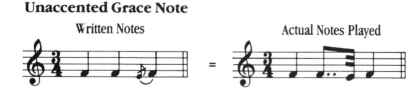

A grace note that features an accent sign is called an *accented grace note* or *appoggiatura*. This note should be played as quickly as possible on the natural beat of the note that follows. Thus, the value of the grace note is deducted from that of the full-sized note, as shown.

Accented Grace Note

Grace notes may also occur in groups. These are usually unaccented grace notes and their time value is deducted from that of the previous beat. A group of two or three grace notes usually features two beams, like sixteenth notes. Groups of four or more grace notes feature three beams, like thirty-second notes. Multiple grace notes should be played quite quickly, according to the skill and taste of the performer.

Trill

A *trill* is an ornament that consists of the rapid alternation of a note with the note above it. A trill lasts for the full length of the indicated note. Here is a quarter note with a trill, and an illustration of how the trill is actually played.

Longer trills usually include a wavy line after the trill symbol.

Tremolo

A *tremolo* is indicated by two half notes joined together with a beam. This means that these two pitches should each be played twice in an alternating pattern of eighth notes.

When half notes are joined with a double beam, the two notes are played four times each in an alternating pattern of sixteenth notes. A triple beam indicates that you play eight alternating thirty-second notes—which, in effect, means to play the alternating pattern as quickly as possible. Tremolos may also be applied to other note values as follows.

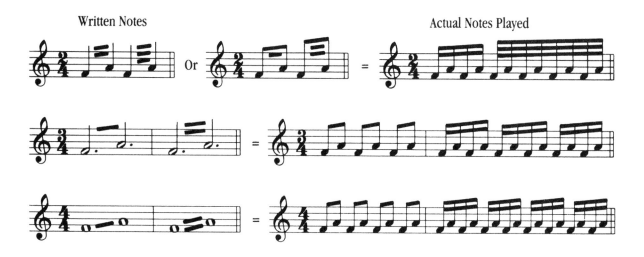

In music for stringed instruments, the term tremolo is used to indicate the rapid repetition of the same note. This figure is indicated with three slash marks through the note's stem, as shown.

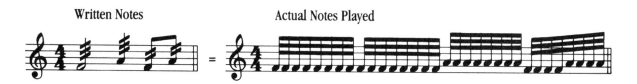

Turns

A *turn* symbol (∾ or ~) placed over a note indicates that a certain pattern of notes should be played or sung, as shown.

If a turn symbol is placed after a note, the pattern begins on the second half of the beat.

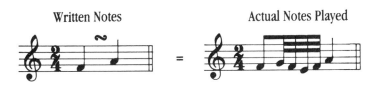

An *inverted turn* is indicated with an inverted turn symbol (∾) and indicates that the turn begin on the note below the written note, as shown. (An inverted turn may also be indicated with the symbols ~ and ℨ.)

If the inverted turn symbol is placed after a note, the pattern begins on the second half of the beat.

Mordents

The *mordent* symbol calls for the quick alternation of the written note with the note above it, as shown. The *lower mordent* calls for the alternation of the written note with the note below it. This ornament appears more commonly than the mordent, which is sometimes called the *upper mordent*.

Upper Mordent   **Lower Mordent**

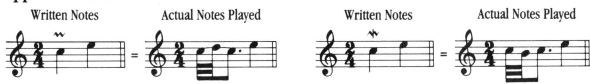

Tempo

The overall speed of a piece of music is called its *tempo*. Variations in tempo are often used to provide contrast in music, particularly in longer works. Composers and arrangers often indicate approximately how fast a piece should be performed by using an Italian or English term on top of the staff at the beginning of a piece or section. Here are some of the more common Italian tempo markings and their English equivalents.

Lento (or **largo**) = Very slow   **Allegretto** = Medium fast
Adagio = Slow   **Allegro** = Fast
Andante = Walking pace   **Presto** = Very fast
Moderato = Medium   **Prestissimo** = As fast as possible

Certain terms call for a changing tempo. The term *rallentando* indicates that the tempo should slow down. *Ritardando* (often abbreviated as *ritard.* or *rit.*) has the same meaning. *Accelerando* calls for a quickening of the tempo. The term *a tempo* tells the musician to return to the normal speed of the piece.

Tempo commodo means that the tempo of the piece is left to the discretion of the performer. *Rubato* indicates that the tempo should speed up and slow down according to taste.

The *metronome* is a device that taps out beats of regular intervals. The metronome's speed may be adjusted, and this makes the device useful to musicians for setting regular and precise tempos during practice. Composers and arrangers may indicate a precise tempo by using a *metronome marking* at the beginning of a piece or section. A metronome marking indicates the note value of the basic beat and the number of beats per minute for the piece. This metronome marking tells us that there are sixty quarter-notes per minute—so each quarter note lasts one second. This is a moderately slow tempo (andante).

Compositions with time signatures that call for a half note, dotted quarter, or eighth note to equal one beat may include metronome markings with these notes. Each of the metronome markings that follow represent a moderate tempo (moderato).

Here are some other examples of metronome markings. From left to right they indicate these tempos: adagio, moderato, allegro, and presto.

Dynamics

Volume is another important factor in musical performance. Terms or symbols that indicate volume are called *dynamic markings.* Italian or English words may be used at the beginning of a piece to indicate overall volume. Symbols are often used to abbreviate these words, especially to indicate volume changes during the piece. Take the time to memorize these common dynamic symbols and their corresponding meanings in Italian and English.

ppp = **Pianississimo** = As soft as possible

pp = **Pianissimo** = Very soft

p = **Piano** = Soft

mp = **Mezzo piano** = Moderately soft

mf = **Mezzo forte** = Moderately loud

f = **Forte** = Loud

ff = **Fortissimo** = Very loud

fff = **Fortississimo** = As loud as possible

Sometimes a composer or arranger wishes to indicate a more gradual change in volume. An increase in volume is indicated by the term *crescendo* (or *cresc.*). The terms *decrescendo* and *diminuendo* (or *dim.*) are used interchangeably to indicate a decrease in volume.

Volume changes may be indicated for specific notes or phrases of a piece by using a *crescendo* or *diminuendo symbol.* A crescendo is traditionally observed in the last four bars of from "For He's a Jolly Good Fellow," as shown in this excerpt. A diminuendo usually occurs after the high note at the end of "O Holy Night." As you can see from these examples, the relative lengths of the lines that form these symbols indicate the notes included in the volume changes.

For He's a Jolly Good Fellow

O Holy Night

Expression

Other Italian and English words are used to indicate that a piece or section be played with a certain expressive quality or feeling. Here are a few of the common Italian and English terms of this kind. Notice that some of these terms also indicate tempo.

Agitato = Agitated

Animato = Animated

Appassionato = With passion

Bravura = Boldly

Brillante = Brilliantly

Cantabile (or **Cantando**) = As if sung

Con anima = With feeling

Con moto = With movement

Con spirito = With spirit

Dolce = Sweetly

Doloroso = Sorrowfully

Energico = Energetically

Espressivo = Expressively

Facile = Easily

Grave = Slow and solemn

Legato = Smoothly

Maestoso = Majestically

Mesto = Sadly

Scherzando = Playfully

Semplice = Simply

Sostenuto = Sustained

Vivace = Lively

You will probably encounter other terms of this kind as you continue your study of written music. It's a good idea to have a music dictionary handy during your study and practice time to look up any terms with which you are unfamiliar.

Guitar Tablature and Notation

This section provides an introduction to written music for the guitar. Here you'll find instructions on reading guitar tablature, including an overview of the symbols used to indicate musical ornaments and playing techniques. You'll also find a detailed discussion of lead sheets and chord charts—the universal musical shorthand for musicians, singers, and songwriters. At the end of this section, there's a brief catalog of popular guitar strum patterns and a useful listing of notes for guitar provided in tablature and standard notation.

Section Contents

Reading Guitar Tablature

Tablature is a well-known system of notation designed specially for guitarists. The tablature staff is composed of six lines. Each line represents a string of the guitar, with string **1** being the highest, and string **6**, the lowest.

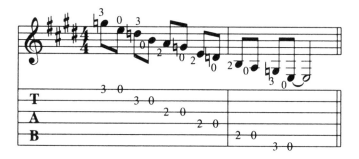

Fret numbers placed on the lines of guitar tablature tell you which fret to play on a given string. (Fret **1** is the fret nearest to the tuning pegs and **0** indicates an unfretted or *open string*.) When fingering numbers are included, they appear with the notes on the staff: 1=index finger, 2=middle finger, 3=ring finger, and 4=pinky.

The first-position *E pentatonic blues scale* is shown below in music notation and guitar tablature. Play this descending scale several times in tempo. Use your middle finger (2) for notes on the second fret and your ring finger (3) for notes on the third fret, as indicated.

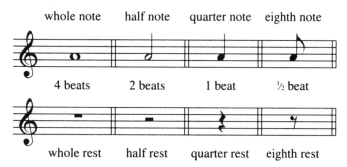

While guitar tablature shows you which frets and strings to play, you must get the rhythm from the notes on the music staff. Here are four standard note values and rests—and their relative duration in beats.

Now play the same descending E pentatonic blues scale in a new rhythmic pattern as you count aloud.

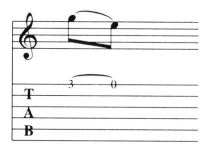

Hammerons, Pulloffs, Slides, and Bends

Hammeron. A slur connecting two ascending notes indicates a hammeron. Play the open first string. While the note is sounding, bring the ring finger (3) of your left hand down at the third fret to play the second note.

Pulloff. A slur connecting two descending notes indicates a pulloff. Fret the first string with your ring finger (3) at the third fret—then play the first note. While the note is still ringing, pluck the string with your left-hand third finger to sound the open-string note.

Slide. A slur and a diagonal line between two notes indicates a slide. Fret the third string with your middle finger (2) at the second fret. Then play the note and quickly slide this finger up the string to the fourth fret.

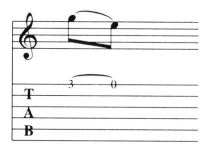

Bend. A slur (with the letter **B**) connecting two notes indicates a bend. Fret the second string with your ring finger (3) at the fifth fret—and play the first note. While the note is sounding, push the string upward to bend the pitch up to the higher note (shown in parentheses).

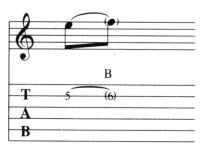

Other Tablature Symbols

Some publications use different symbols to notate bends. These are shown below, along with a few other symbols indicating other common playing techniques.

SEMI-TONE BEND: Strike the note and bend up a semi-tone (1/2 step).

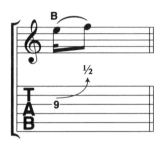

WHOLE-TONE BEND: Strike the note and bend up a whole-tone (whole step).

GRACE NOTE BEND: Strike the note and bend as indicated. Play the first note as quickly as possible.

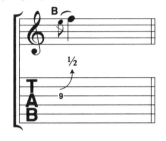

QUARTER-TONE BEND: Strike the note and bend up a 1/4 step.

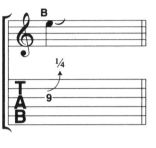

BEND & RELEASE: Strike the note and bend up as indicated, then release back to the original note.

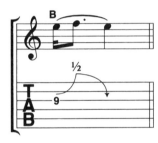

BEND & RESTRIKE: Strike the note and bend as indicated then restrike the string where the symbol occurs.

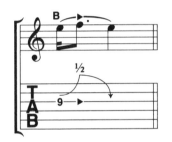

PRE-BEND: Bend the note as indicated, then strike it.

PRE-BEND & RELEASE: Bend the note as indicated. Strike it and release the note back to the original pitch.

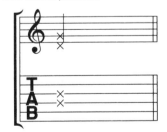

NATURAL HARMONIC: Strike the note while the fret-hand lightly touches the string directly over the fret indicated.

PICK SCRAPE: The edge of the pick is rubbed down (or up) the string, producing a scratchy sound.

PALM MUTING: The note is partially muted by the pick hand lightly touching the string(s) just before the bridge.

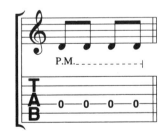

MUFFLED STRINGS: A percussive sound is produced by laying the fret hand across the string(s) without depressing, and striking them with the pick hand.

NOTE: The speed of any bend is indicated by the music notation and tempo.

Lead Sheets

A *lead sheet* is a written version of a song that contains the melody, chords, and lyrics. Take a look at the rock/blues song "Crossroads" notated in lead-sheet form.

A) Title. The title appears at the top and center of the first page of the lead sheet. When creating your own lead sheet, use initial capitals on all title words with four letters or more. Always use initial capitals on the first and last word of a title. Don't capitalize articles ("a," "an," and "the"), conjunctions ("and" and "but"), or prepositions ("on," "in," "out," and so on). Capitalize prepositions that are part of a verbal phrase (as in "Roll Out the Barrel"). Avoid subtitles or alternate titles that detract from your phrase of choice.

B) Lyricist/Composer. Use initial capitals to credit the lyricist and composer. If the words and music are created by one person, write "Words and music by [name]" in this position.

C) Tempo/Feel. Indicate the tempo or feel of a song in this position. Here, a simple instruction like "Medium rock" or "Slow shuffle" is often most useful. Only the first word of the tempo indication should be capitalized.

D) Treble Clef. Except in special cases, a lead sheet should be notated in the treble clef. This clef should appear at the beginning of every staff line.

D) Key Signature. The sharps and flats indicating the key appear at the beginning of every staff of the lead sheet.

E) Time Signature. The time signature is written after the key signature at the beginning of the first staff only.

F) Riff Figure. Some of the songs you write may feature an important instrumental riff as an integral part of the song structure. A riff may occur at any point during the song. In this example, the riff figure forms the introduction. Don't feel the need to add a riff figure to your lead sheet unless it really needs one. Many riffs should be saved for inclusion in the full arrangement of a song.

G) Melody. The complete melody of the song should be clearly notated on the staff. There's no need to write special instructions to the vocalist or notate melody nuances that can be worked out later. The melody should be notated in its simplest form.

H) Lyric. Each syllable of the lyric should correspond with one or more melody notes. Hyphens divide words into syllables. If one syllable lasts for more than one note, the hyphen is centered under the corresponding melody notes. If a word (or the last syllable of a word) is held for two melody notes, it is followed by a horizontal underline. One or two extra verses may be included beneath the first verse (in which case, the verses should be numbered "1," "2," "3," and so on). Some songs feature more than one or two extra verses. These should appear at the bottom of the lead sheet in block text (and numbered "2," "3," "4," and so on).

I) Chord Symbols. The lead sheet includes chord letter names outlining the harmonic structure of a song. Try not to use unnecessarily complex chords here. Just reduce the harmony to its simple important movements.

J) Section Labels. It's helpful to include song section labels—like *Introduction, Verse, Chorus,* and *Tag*—to clarify the overall structure of the song.

K) Copyright Notice. Your song is protected by copyright law as soon as it is written. It's a good idea to include a copyright notice at the bottom of your lead sheet with the year and the name of the song's rightful owner.

Chord Charts

A *chord chart* is an arrangement of a song that contains chord symbols only. Take a look at the chord chart for the rock/blues song "Crossroads." A basic chord chart like the one that follows need only show the general outline of the harmony: the name and duration of each chord. Here, four slash marks in each measure represent the four quarter-note beats per measure of $\frac{4}{4}$ time.

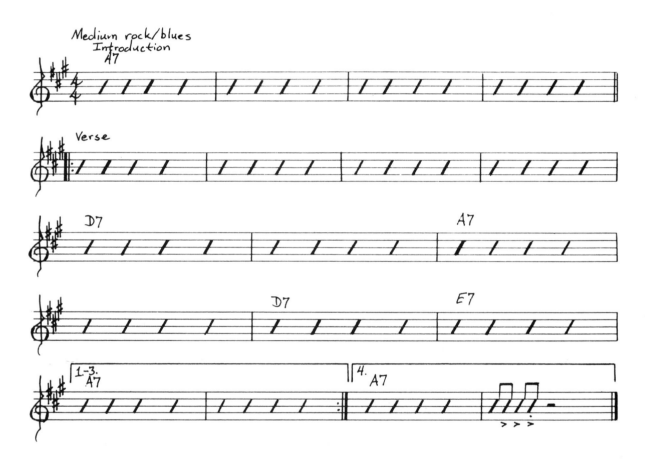

Transposing Chords

The most commonly used chords in any major key are those built on the first, fourth, and fifth degrees of the scale. These are often referred to as *I*, *IV*, and *V7* *chords.* If you know the I, IV, and V7 chords in every key, then you know the chords to thousands of songs. Here is a chart of these chords for quick reference.

I	IV	V7		I	IV	V7
C	F	G7		Gb	Cb	Db 7
C#	F#	G#7		G	C	D7
Db	Gb	Ab 7		Ab	Db	Eb 7
D	G	A7		A	D	E7
Eb	Ab	Bb 7		Bb	Eb	F7
E	A	B7		B	E	F#7
F	Bb	C7		Cb	Fb	Gb 7
F#	B	C#7				

Rhythmic Notation

Sometimes it is convenient to combine chord-chart and lead-sheet notation to produce a more complete picture of a guitar arrangement. In this case, the chord notation may be written above the lead line to convey the strumming pattern to the guitarist. You will often see this type of arrangement in guitar songbooks. Rhythmic notation of this kind is also sometimes used in guitar tablature arrangements or transcriptions to notate a rhythm guitar part.

Below are several examples of how basic strum notation is used to enhance a standard lead sheet.

The Bass-Chord Strum

For this strum, play a single bass note on beats one and three and strum only on beats two and four: bass-chord-bass-chord. For the A chord, use the open A string (⑤) for the bass notes. For the E7 chord, use the open low E string (⑥).

Tom Dooley

The Bass-Chord-Chord Strum

This example is in ¾ time, or waltz time. Since there are three quarter-note beats per measure, this pattern uses a single bass note followed by two strums.

Clementine

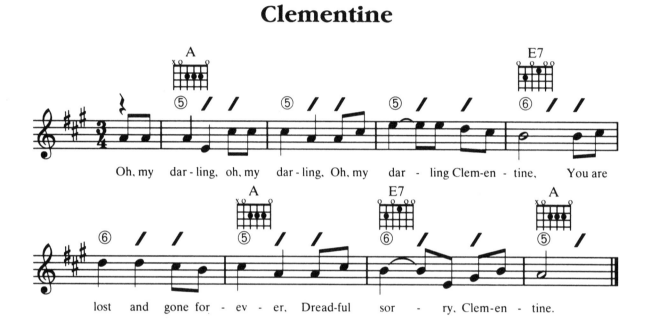

Oh, my   dar - ling, oh, my   dar - ling, Oh, my   dar - ling Clem-en - tine,   You are

lost   and   gone for - ev - er, Dread-ful   sor - ry, Clem-en - tine.

The Alternating Bass-Chord Strum

In these types of simple strumming patterns, it is common to alternate the bass notes between a *primary bass* and a *secondary bass.* For the A chord, the secondary bass will be the open sixth string (⑥). While holding down the E7 chord, use the fifth string (⑤) fretted at the second fret as the secondary bass.

Old Joe Clark

Old Joe Clark, he   had   a   house,   Six - teen sto - ries   high,
I went down to   Old Joe's house,   Old Joe was not   home,

Ev - ery sto - ry   in   that house,   Full   of   chick - en   pie.
I   ate   all   of   Old Joe's meat,   Left Old   Joe __ the   bone.

Fare thee well, ____   Old   Joe   Clark,   Fare thee well,   I   say

Fare thee well, ____   Old   Joe   Clark,   Ain't got   long   to   stay.
I'm   a - go-in' a -   way.

Eighth-Note Strums

Here are some more complex strumming patterns that make use of eighth notes. To play these patterns fingerstyle, flick down and up across the strings with your index or middle finger. If you are using a pick, follow the downstroke (⊓) and upstroke (∨) indications. On the downstroke, try to cover all of the strings except the primary bass note. On the upstroke, strum lightly across only two or three strings.

Old Joe Clark

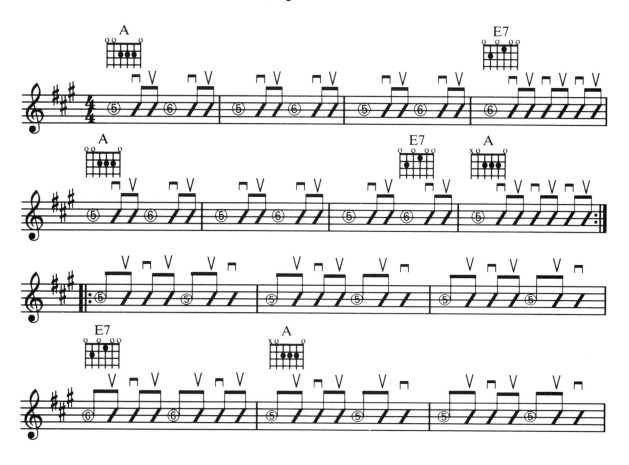

Eighth-Note Strums in ¾ Time

The following example shows several variations on eighth-note strums in waltz time. Each measure features one bass note on the downbeat in true waltz fashion. In the fifth and sixth measures, the chord changes on the third beat of each measure to provide added movement to the piece.

Drink to Me Only With Thine Eyes

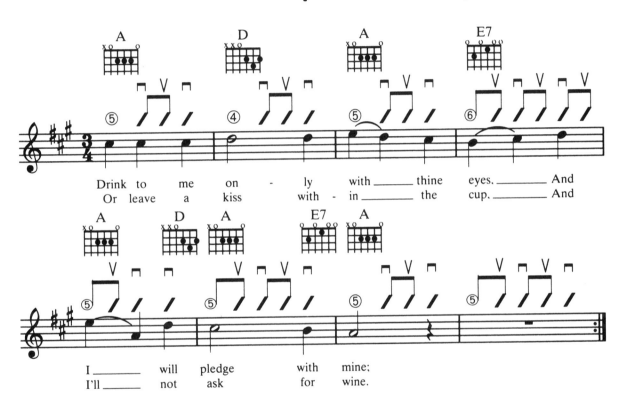

Syncopated Rhythms

Syncopation is an important rhythmic technique used in all kinds of music, especially jazz and rock. Simply speaking, a syncopated strum is an eighth-note strum in which you leave out some of the downstrokes. This has the effect of accenting the upstrokes, which fall on the *offbeats*.

Two different syncopated patterns are notated in "Sloop *John B.*" below. In the verse, full strums are called for. The chorus uses a bass-chord type strum with only one bass note per measure. Notice that the patterns are only shown for one or two bars when they first appear or when the bass note changes. This usually means that the indicated strumming pattern is just a suggestion—and that the player is free to play variations at will.

Sloop John B.

Table of Notes

This chart shows all of the notes in *first position* (the first four frets) plus the notes on the first string up to the twelfth fret. The natural and sharp notes, along with their letter names, are on top. The enharmonic equivalents of the sharp notes are shown on the bottom line.

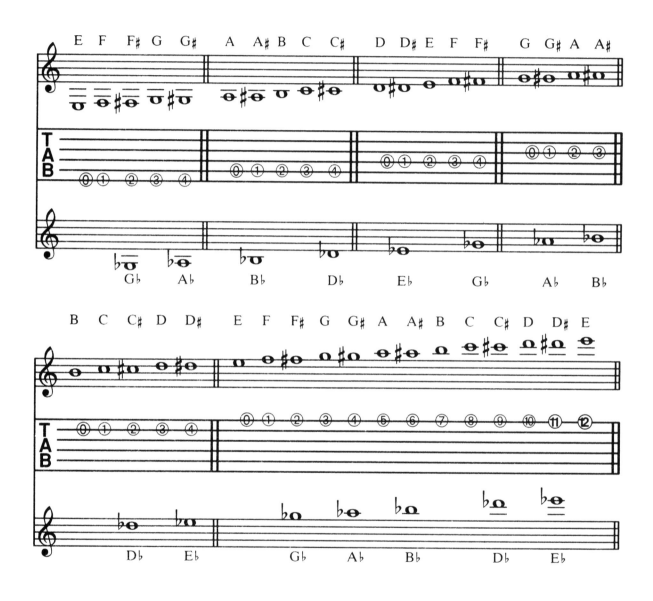

 # Book 3

Guitar Scale Dictionary

Scales can do wonders for your playing if you practice them regularly—and if you understand how the different types of scales are constructed. The more scales you are familiar with, the more choices you'll have when building riffs for an arrangement or improvised solo.

The first section of this book provides a guitarist's guide to scale theory. This is followed by a comprehensive listing of all common and advanced scales in guitar tablature. Here you will find standard, altered, embellished, and open-string scales—as well as some truly exotic scales from different cultures.

Basic Scale Theory

While it is important to know how to play a variety of scales, it is equally important to understand how these scales are constructed. This section offers some background on the inner workings of common scale types as well as information on how they are used in various musical contexts.

Section Contents

Major Scales and Key Signatures

Simply defined, a scale is a series of tones organized according to a specific arrangement of *intervals*. An interval is the distance between any two tones, or pitches. The smallest interval (excepting the *unison*) is the *half step*, which corresponds to the difference in pitch between two notes one fret apart on the same string.

A distance of two half-steps is, naturally, a *whole step*.

Any scale may be defined exclusively by its arrangement of whole and half steps. If you know a scale's formula of whole and half steps, you can construct that scale beginning on any note. For example, examine the layout of the major scale below.

C major scale (⌣ = whole step ⌣ = half step)

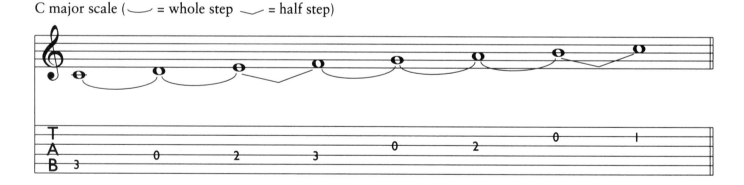

The formula of whole-whole-half-whole-whole-whole-half is the same for any major scale.

If you look at the C major scale above in two halves, you can see that each half has the same formula of whole and half steps—that is, whole-whole-half—and that the two halves are separated by one whole-step. From what you know about scale formulas, this means that the second half of the C major scale can start off a new major scale. Since this new scale will begin on G, it is said to have a *tonal center* of G, or, more simply, to be a G major scale.

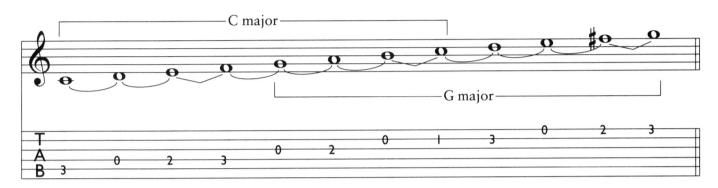

Notice that to keep the arrangement of whole and half steps the same as it was in the C major scale, the seventh degree of the G major scale must be sharped. Since the formula must be consistent, the G major scale will always contain an F♯. Because the scale always contains an F♯, the *key signature* of the key of G major is written like this:

Let's now take the second half of the G scale and use it as the first half of a new major scale. Notice that we have dropped the G major scale down an octave to put the new scale in a more easily playable range.

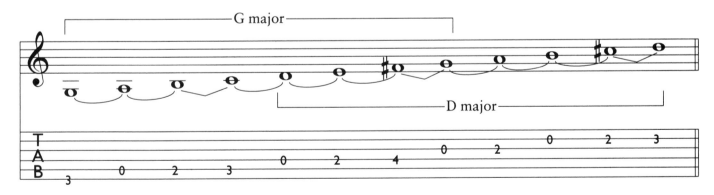

In the same way that the F♯ was added to the G scale, a C♯ must be added to the D scale to make it agree with the major scale formula. This means that the key signature of D major contains two sharps, F and C.

Continuing this process of taking the second half of a major scale to be the first half of the next will produce twelve distinct major scales each with its own distinct key signature. Notice that it is necessary to use flats rather than sharps to produce the scales in the second column of the following chart.

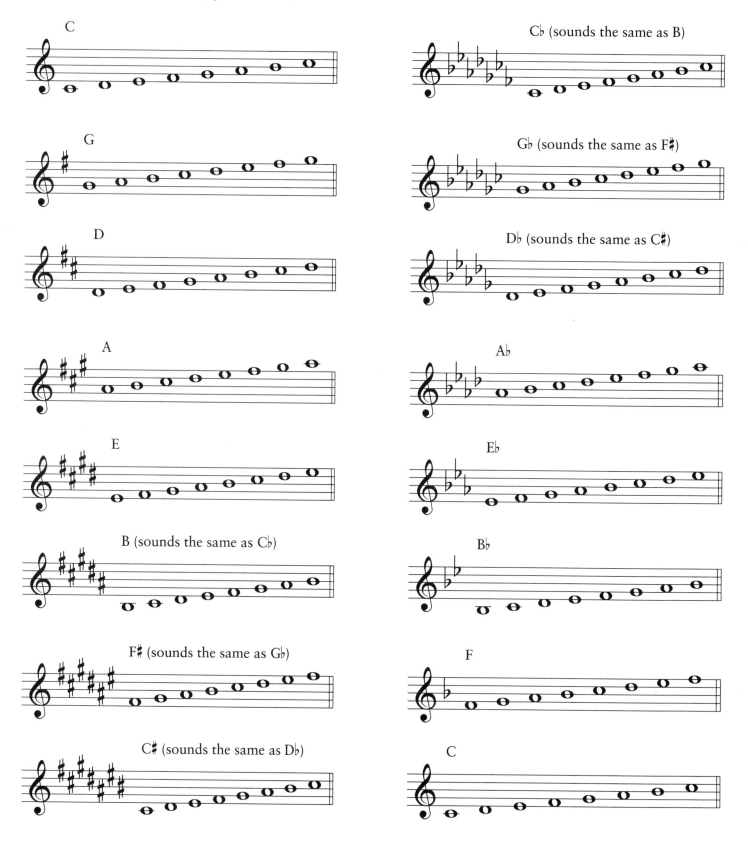

Although it is not necessary to memorize any of the foregoing material in order to make use of the scales and exercises in this book, having this information at your fingertips—as well as any other music theory you can pick up—can only help your playing.

The Circle of Fifths

The order in which the scales are presented in the chart above is referred to as the *circle of fifths*. It is a circle because it starts and ends at the key of C. It is the circle of fifths because each scale begins on the fifth degree of its preceding scale, or the interval of a perfect fifth above. This relationship of the twelve major scales may be expressed in the following circle diagram.

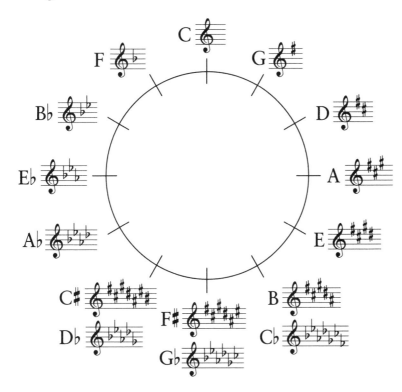

Minor Scales and Key Signatures

Every one of the major scales has a corresponding *relative minor* scale that shares the same key signature. You can find the starting note of a major scale's relative minor scale by going up to the sixth degree of that major scale. Thus, the relative minor of C major is A minor.

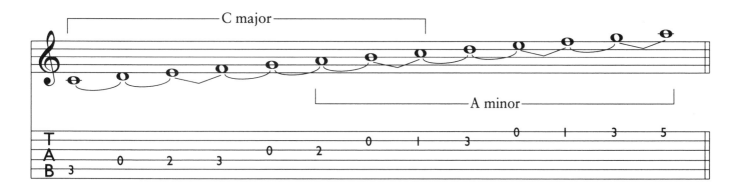

Here is a chart showing all of the relative minor scales.

Major Key	Relative Minor
C Major (no sharps or flats)	A Minor
G Major (one sharp: F♯)	E Minor
D Major (two sharps: F♯, C♯)	B Minor
A Major (three sharps: F♯, C♯, G♯)	F-sharp Minor
E Major (four sharps: F♯, C♯, G♯, D♯)	C-sharp Minor
B Major (five sharps: F♯, C♯, G♯, D♯, A♯)	G-sharp Minor
F-sharp Major (six sharps: F♯, C♯, G♯, D♯, A♯, E♯)	D-sharp Minor
C-sharp Major (seven sharps: F♯, C♯, G♯, D♯, A♯, E♯, B♯)	A-sharp Minor
F Major (one flat: B♭)	D Minor
B-flat Major (two flats: B♭, E♭)	G Minor
E-flat Major (three flats: B♭, E♭, A♭)	C Minor
A-flat Major (four flats: B♭, E♭, A♭, D♭)	F Minor
D-flat Major (five flats: B♭, E♭, A♭, D♭, G♭)	B-flat Minor
G-flat Major (six flats: B♭, E♭, A♭, D♭, G♭, C♭)	E-flat Minor
C-flat Major (seven flats: B♭, E♭, A♭, D♭, G♭, C♭, F♭)	A-flat Minor

Harmonic and Melodic Minor Scales

The relative minor scales referred to above are known as *natural minor* scales because they occur naturally, without deviating from their key signatures. These scales are commonly altered to form *harmonic minor* and *melodic minor* scales. The harmonic minor scale is formed by raising the seventh degree of a natural minor.

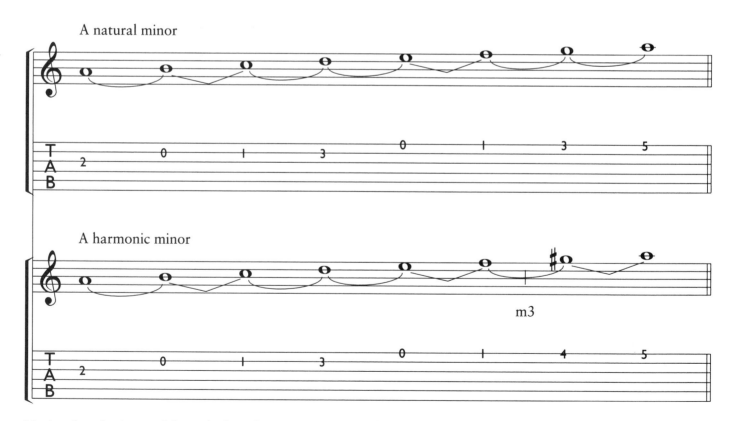

Notice that the interval formula for a harmonic minor scale includes one interval that is neither a whole step nor a half step. The *minor third*, abbreviated *m3*, is equal to three half-steps.

The other common type of minor scale is the *melodic minor* scale, produced by raising the sixth and seventh degrees of the natural minor scale.

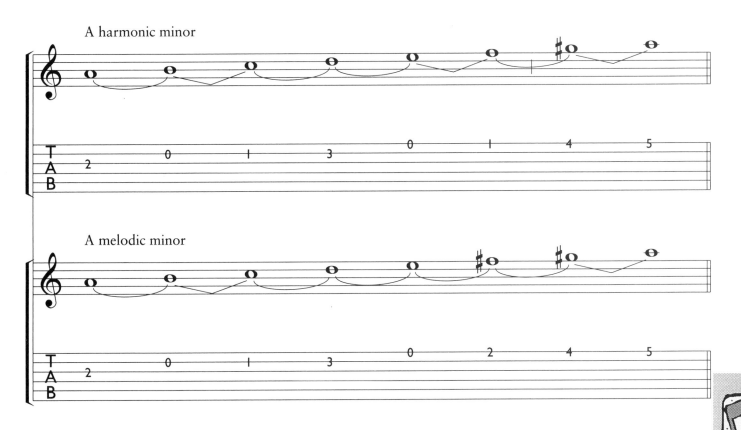

Notice that the second half of the interval formula of a melodic minor scale is identical to that of a major scale. In fact, the only difference between a melodic minor scale and a major scale is the third degree.

Traditionally, the melodic minor scale form is said to follow the formula of the natural minor when descending.

In recent times, it has become theoretically preferable to retain the same formula descending as ascending. Most people who think of the melodic minor in this way refer to it as a *jazz melodic minor* to distinguish it from the traditional interpretation. You will only find forms for the traditional melodic minor presented in the pages that follow, but you may easily practice jazz melodic minors by simply applying the same fingering going down as you do going up.

Modes

Modes are produced by displacing the starting point of a scale without changing its interval formula. This has the effect of turning out a scale with a new arrangement of whole and half steps. Most often, when musicians talk about modes they are referring to the seven modes of the major scale, although modes may be generated from any scale at all.

The modes are known by their Greek names (which were given to them by some rather creative Medieval theoreticians and have very little to do with Greece or Greek music).

The Dorian Mode

Starting on the second degree of a major scale yields a *Dorian* scale. This scale is very useful in jazz and jazz/rock—in which it is used for soloing over minor seventh chords—and sounds like the natural minor with a raised sixth.

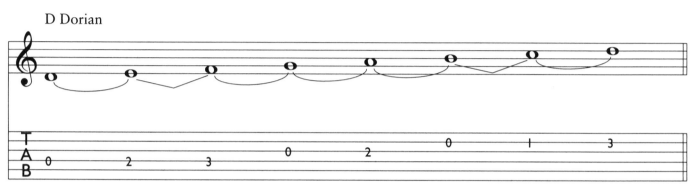

The Phrygian Mode

Playing a C major from E to E gives us an E *Phrygian* scale; reminiscent of flamenco music and sounding like the natural minor with a flatted second.

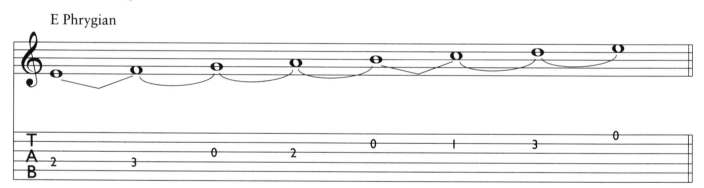

The Lydian Mode

The mode starting on the fourth degree of the major scale is known as a *Lydian* scale. This one has a major sound but differs from a straight major scale in its sharped fourth. In jazz, Lydian mode scales are generally used for soloing over major seventh chords other than the I chord.

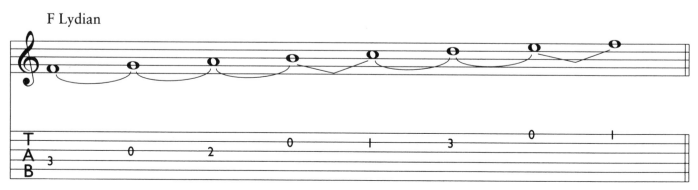

The Mixolydian Mode

Starting on the fifth degree of a major scale produces another major-sounding scale, the *Mixolydian* mode; this time with a flatted seventh. You will hear this one a lot in folk and rock music.

G Mixolydian

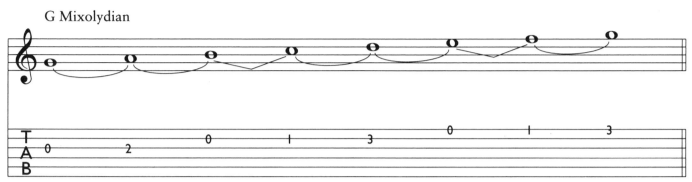

The Aeolian Mode

Remember that starting on the sixth degree of a major scale produces its relative minor. In the terminology of the modes, major is called *Ionian* and natural minor, *Aeolian*.

The Locrian Mode

The seventh mode, *Locrian,* was avoided for centuries due to its truly weird flavor. Because the scale outlines a diminished chord, melodies written in the Locrian mode never seem to quite come to rest. Inasmuch as this is sometimes a desirable quality in modern music, this mode has come into its own during the twentieth century. Also, the Locrian is useful in jazz soloing where it is commonly used over minor seventh flat-five (half-diminished) chords.

B Locrian

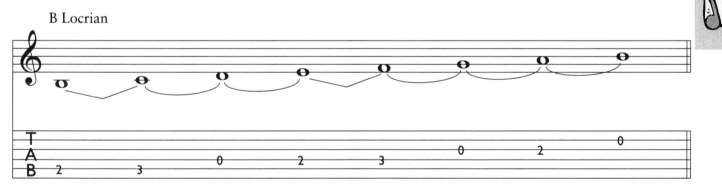

Chromatic Scales

A *chromatic* scale is the simplest example of a type of scale known as a *symmetrical* scale. The formula for a chromatic scale is simply all half steps.

Chromatic scale

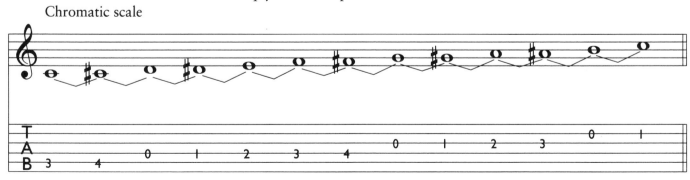

Because the intervals between notes are all identical, any note in the scale may be considered its root: no matter where you start, the formula will come out the same.

Rock Scales

Major Pentatonic Scales

In addition to the usual major, minor, and modal scales, much rock music is based on five-note scales called *pentatonic* scales. The basic form of pentatonic scale is the major pentatonic built from the first, second, third, fifth, and sixth degrees of a major scale. This scale is often heard in Southern rock, rhythm and blues, country music, and light rock.

C major pentatonic scale

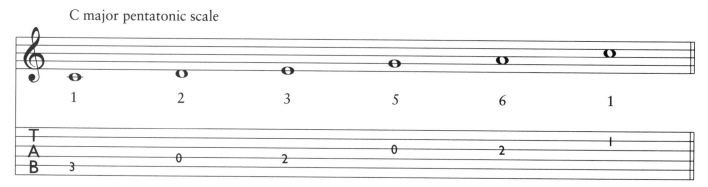

Minor Pentatonic, or Blues, Scales

By taking the relative minor of the major pentatonic scale, you can produce a *minor pentatonic,* or *blues,* scale. Thus the C major pentatonic above becomes an A blues scale by starting it on A.

A minor pentatonic (blues) scale

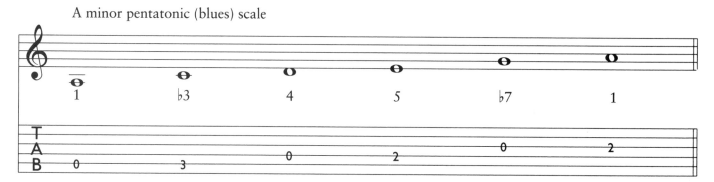

The reason that the minor pentatonic scale is good for blues lies in its flatted third—flatted in comparison to the third of the major scale. In blues—and, consequently in most rock—the third degree is often ambiguous; neither major nor minor, but somewhere in between. On guitar, this effect is easy to produce with string bending.

In addition to the ambiguous "blue" third, the pentatonic blues scale is commonly ornamented by adding the normal major third and the flatted fifth.

A blues scale with major third and flatted fifth

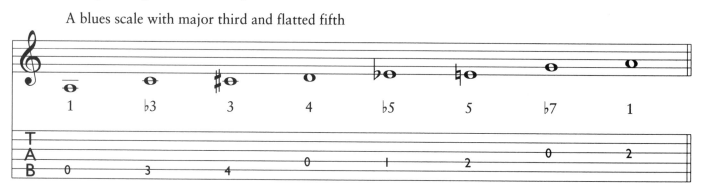

Jazz Scales

There are many theories concerning the application of scales to jazz improvisation—some say there are as many theories as there are jazz players. The brief descriptions of how the following scales are commonly used should not therefore be taken as gospel, but rather as springboards to your further investigation of jazz theory.

Jazz Melodic Minor Scales

As stated above, a *jazz melodic minor* scale is nothing more than a traditional melodic minor scale with the same formula descending as ascending (see "Minor Scales" above). The jazz melodic minor scale may be used to generate the *Lydian flat-seven* scale (see below).

Lydian Flat-Seven Scales

The *Lydian flat-seven* scale is generally used for soloing over dominant seventh chords other than the V chord of the progression (for which the Mixolydian scale usually suffices). The formula of the scale reveals it to be a cross between a Mixolydian and a Lydian scale, containing a flatted seventh and a sharped fourth (as compared to a major scale). This scale may also be thought of as the Lydian mode of the jazz melodic minor.

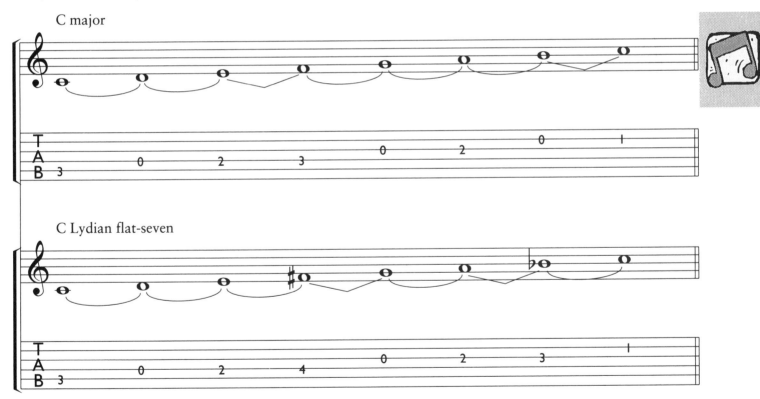

Diminished Scales

Like the chromatic scale, the *diminished* scale is a symmetrical scale, in that more than one note in the scale may be considered the root. Since its formula is a repeating alternation of whole-step/half-step, starting on every other degree will yield three other scales with identical formulas. Because of this, the C diminished scale shown below could also be considered an E-flat diminished scale, a G-flat diminished scale, or an A diminished scale.

C diminished scale

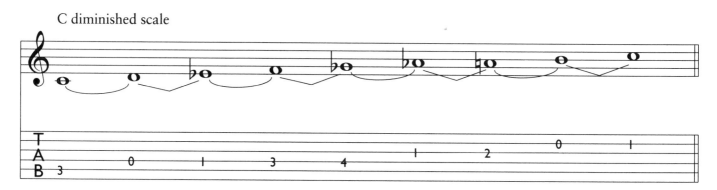

In addition to being used to solo over diminished seventh chords, the diminished scale is often used over dominant seventh chords to add tensions (flat-nine, sharp-nine, sharp-eleven, and thirteen). When used in this way, the root of the diminished scale should be one half-step above the root of the seventh chord.

Whole-Tone Scales

Another symmetrical scale is the *whole-tone* scale. Where the formula of the chromatic scale comprises all half steps and that of the diminished scale consists of alternating whole and half steps, all intervals in the whole-tone scale are whole steps.

C whole-tone scale

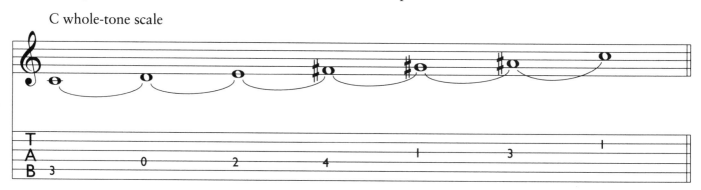

This scale goes well with augmented seventh chords because it contains all the tones of the chord plus the ninth and the sharped eleventh.

Altered Scales

Combining the first half of the diminished scale with the second half of the whole-tone scale (one half-step above) yields the *altered* scale, used against dominant seventh chords altered with the tensions flat-five, sharp-five, flat-nine, sharp-nine, and/or sharp eleven.

C altered scale

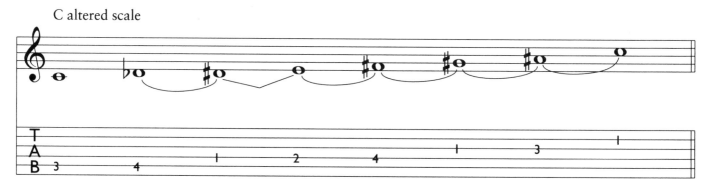

Notice that the formula of the diminished-scale portion of the C altered scale above shows it to be based on a D-flat diminished scale, even though it starts on C, a half step below. Notice also that while the diminished scale has eight steps per octave and the whole-tone scale only six, the altered scale has seven steps per octave just like the standard major, minor, and modal scales.

Basic Scales

This section includes fingerings for scales used in every style of guitar music. Even though the scales are divided into the categories like "Rock Scales" and "Jazz Scales," the material here is designed to be general and nature, and so it may apply to just about any style of contemporary music.

Section Contents

In-Position Major Scales

These scales are remarkably versatile tools. They give you seven starting points for basic major scales within one position on the neck. They are all moveable forms (containing no open strings), and each one covers a little over two octaves. If you really have a command of these forms, you will find that you can play any major (or modal) scale within one fret of any position you may be in. Note that although each of these stays within one four-fret position, some of them contain stretches up with the fourth finger or down with the first finger. These stretches are indicated by the letter *s*.

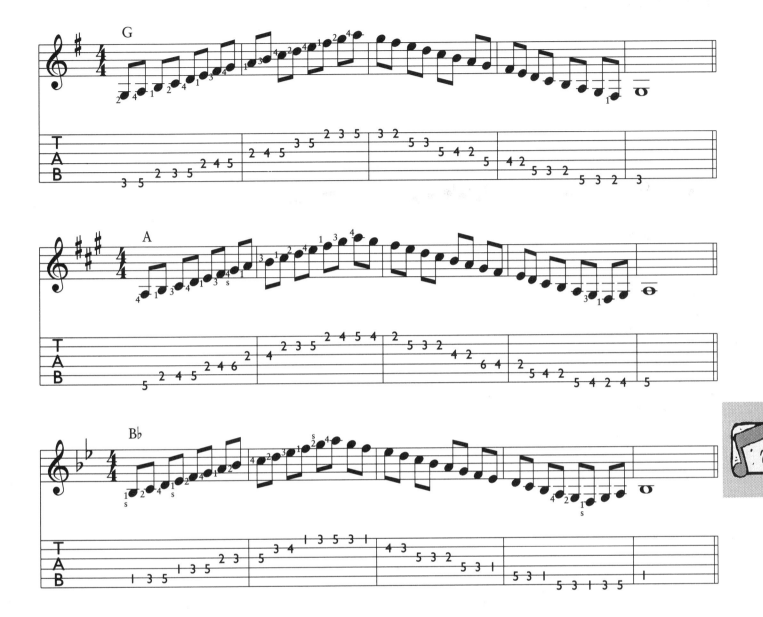

Here's an idea for practicing these scales that will really get them under your fingers: Play each scale form starting from the same root. For example, if you were to start from G-flat, the C scale form would be moved to eighth position, the D scale form to sixth position, the E-flat to fifth position, and so on. This would give you the G-flat scale in all seven positions.

In-Position Minor Scales

Any of the major-scale forms above may be transformed into a natural minor scale by simply starting on the sixth degree; thus C major becomes A natural minor, D major becomes B minor, E-flat major becomes C minor, and so on. Since the harmonic and melodic minor scale forms require different fingerings, they are written out below.

Harmonic Minor Scales

To produce harmonic minor scales, you simply sharp the seventh degree.

A harmonic minor

B harmonic minor

C harmonic minor

D harmonic minor

E harmonic minor

F# harmonic minor

G harmonic minor

Melodic Minor Scales

Remember that there are two kinds of melodic minor scales and that the forms in this book are of the "traditional" variety. If you want to practice jazz melodic minor scales, use the same fingering descending as ascending.

A melodic minor

B melodic minor

C melodic minor

D melodic minor

E melodic minor

F♯ melodic minor

Chromatic Scales

Since the chromatic scale has no real tonal center, there is no need to present forms with different starting points. The following two forms differ only in fingering.

Chromatic

Rock Scales

You can derive pentatonic scales from any major or minor scale by just taking the appropriate five tones and leaving out the rest (as outlined above in the "Scale Theory" section). The following are the most often used forms of these scales.

Major Pentatonic Scales

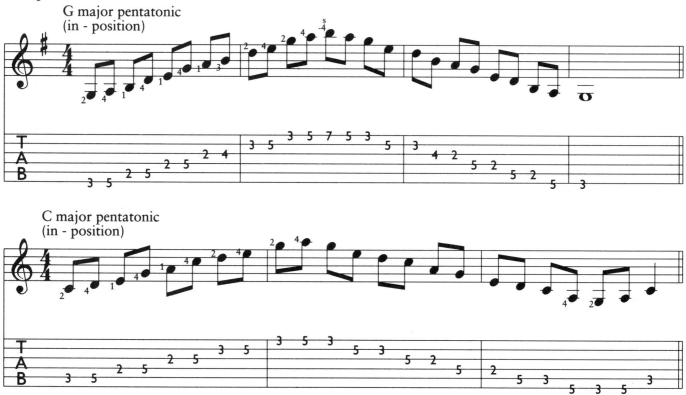

G major pentatonic
(in - position)

C major pentatonic
(in - position)

G major pentatonic
(with position shifts)

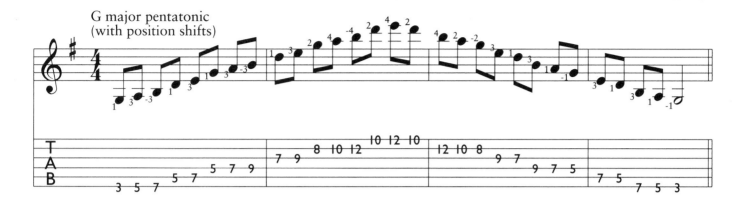

C major pentatonic
(with position shifts)

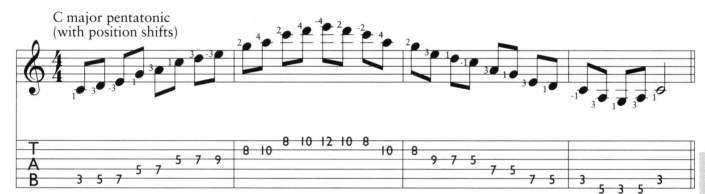

Minor Pentatonic Scales

G minor pentatonic
(in - position)

C minor pentatonic
(in - position)

E minor pentatonic
(with position shifts)

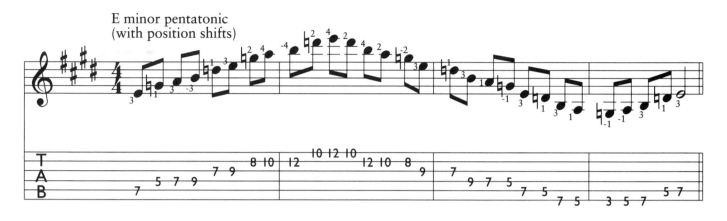

A minor pentatonic
(with position shifts)

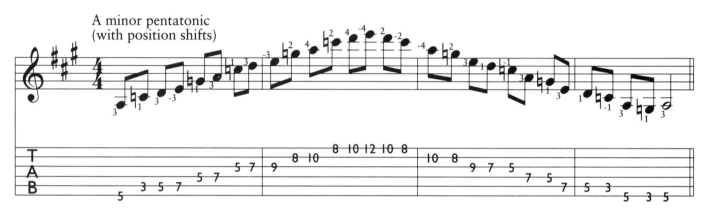

Blues Scales with Major Third and Flatted Fifth

G blues scale with major third and flatted fifth
(in - position)

C blues scale with major third and flatted fifth
(in - position)

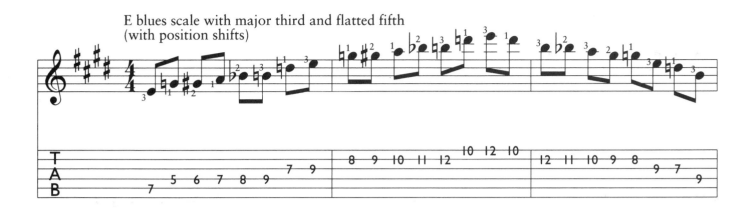

E blues scale with major third and flatted fifth
(with position shifts)

A blues scale with major third and flatted fifth
(with position shifts)

Jazz Scales

Since the jazz melodic minor scale is so similar to the traditional melodic minor, it is not necessary to detail any new forms for it. Let's take a look at the Lydian mode of the jazz melodic minor, known as the Lydian flat-seven.

Lydian Flat-Seven Scales

Compare these in-position forms to the melodic minor forms given above to understand their modal connection.

C Lydian flat-seven

G Lydian flat-seven

Diminished Scales

Here are two common in-position fingerings and one "sliding scale" fingering for the diminished scale. Remember that every other note may be considered the root, so practice these forms with different starting points to learn them thoroughly.

G, B♭, C♯, or E diminished

C, E♭, G♭, or A diminished

G, B♭, C♯, or E diminished

Whole-Tone Scales

Since the whole-tone scale has a perfectly symmetrical formula, what was said about the diminished scales above goes double here: Practice these forms considering each and every scale tone as the root.

G, A, B, C#, D#, or F whole-tone

C, D, E, G♭, A♭, or B♭ whole-tone

G, A, B, C#, D#, or F whole-tone

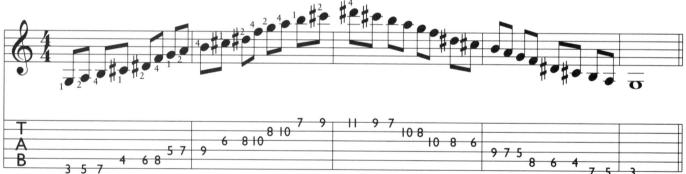

Altered Scales

Here are good in-position patterns for altered scales.

C altered

G altered

C altered

Advanced Scales

The scale patterns in this section are for the most part more exotic than the basic scales in the preceding section. Many of these scales are used in blues, jazz, and rock improvisation, while some are identified more frequently with folk and classical music. Certain scale patterns are specifically designed to improve your strength and facility over the entire length of the fingerboard. Other advanced scales involve special techniques, such as tap-ons, harmonics, or the use of open strings. For those interested in progressive and "world" musics, there are also some fascinating scales from Africa, Eastern Europe, India, Malaysia, and Japan.

Section Contents

Tonal Pentatonic Scales

A tonal pentatonic scale is a five-note scale that has no half-tones. The most commonly used scale of this kind is called the *major pentatonic scale*—and is often heard in country and rock music. Note that this scale is based on the major scale (minus the fourth and seventh degrees).

C Major Pentatonic Scale

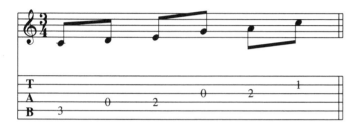

Four additional pentatonic modes may be derived from the major pentatonic scale by starting on each scale degree in turn. Here's a brief description of the tonal pentatonic modes. These scales occur in the music of many cultures and periods—from the ancient melodies of the Celts, Chinese, and Aztecs to today's most sophisticated rock and jazz improvisations.

Tonal Pentatonic Scale 2. Begins on the second degree of the pentatonic scale. This scale commonly occurs in "old-timey" folk music of the American Southeast. Contemporary bluegrass and country musicians often use this mode to evoke this haunting, traditional sound.

Tonal Pentatonic Scale 3. Begins on the third degree of the major pentatonic scale. Because of its ambiguous tonal center, this unusual scale has limited use.

Tonal Pentatonic Scale 4. Begins on the fourth degree of the pentatonic scale. This form is sometimes considered the "true" tonal pentatonic scale. It occurs in ancient music around the globe, but has limited use in usual contemporary settings. However, it can be heard in avant-garde, new age, and "world" musics that reflect African, Asian, or Celtic influences.

Tonal Pentatonic Scale 5. Also known as the *minor pentatonic scale* (or *pentatonic blues scale*), this form begins on the fifth degree of the major pentatonic scale. This scale is the basis for most traditional blues music—and naturally occurs in today's blues-based jazz and rock. This scale (along with its six-note and seven-note forms) is discussed more fully in the section "Blues Scale Variations."

D Tonal Pentatonic Scale 2

E Tonal Pentatonic Scale 3

G Tonal Pentatonic Scale 4

A Tonal Pentatonic Scale 5
(also known as Minor Pentatonic *or* Pentatonic Blues*)*

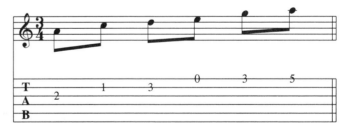

Because the tonal pentatonic scales may be used with a wide variety of chords and progressions, they allow for a good deal of melodic freedom. For this reason, modern songwriters and improvisers use these scales to evoke a powerful ethnic or avant-garde sound, particularly in an alternative jazz or new age context. Once you are familiar with the above scales, explore the modes derived from another major pentatonic scale in a different key, such as A or D.

You can derive fingerings for pentatonic scales from basic major-scale patterns. To play a major pentatonic scale, just leave out the fourth and seventh degrees of the parallel major scale fingering pattern. This fingering may also be used to play the four modes of the major pentatonic scale by starting on each scale degree in turn. Here are the four most useful fingerings for tonal pentatonic scales (based on major-scale fingering Types 1, 2, 5, and 6, respectively).

Type 1

Type 2

Type 5

Type 6

Semitonal Pentatonic Scales

A *semitonal pentatonic scale* is a five-note scale that includes half steps. Technically there are two such scales. The first one is produced by omitting the second and sixth degree of the major scale.

C Semitonal Pentatonic Scale

Like the tonal pentatonic scale, this semitonal pentatonic scale has four "modes," as shown.

E Semitonal Pentatonic Scale 2

F Semitonal Pentatonic Scale 3

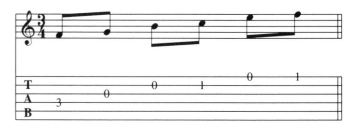

G Semitonal Pentatonic Scale 4

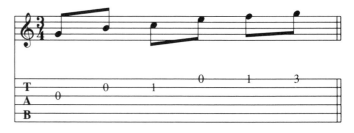

B Semitonal Pentatonic Scale 5

Fingering patterns for semitonal pentatonic scales may be derived from major-scale fingerings. So, to produce the first semitonal pentatonic scale given above, omit the second and sixth degrees of the parallel major scale. This fingering may also be used to play the four modes of this scale by starting on each scale degree in turn. (As with tonal pentatonic scales, the four fingering types which work best for semitonal pentatonic scales are based on major-scale fingering Types 1, 2, 5, and 6.)

The second (or alternate) form of semitonal pentatonic scale is produced by omitting the second and fifth degrees of the major scale. Once you are familiar with this scale, try playing its four modes by beginning on each scale degree in turn.

C Semitonal Pentatonic Scale (Alternate)

As a general rule, semitonal pentatonic scales add a strong dissonant flavor to guitar solos and arrangements. These unusual scales (and their variations) are usually associated with the musics of specific cultures. For this reason, their harmonic applications depend upon their idiomatic contexts—and can not be discussed in general terms.

Several more interesting semitonal pentatonic scales are included in the section "Ethnic Scales" at the end of this book.

Jazz Melodic Minor Scales

As its name implies, the *jazz melodic minor scale* is a variation of the melodic minor scale commonly used in traditional and modern jazz music. As compared to the major scale, the standard melodic minor scale features a lowered 3rd when ascending—and a lowered 3rd, 6th, and 7th when descending. The jazz melodic minor simply uses the ascending melodic minor form for both ascending and descending passages.

Composers and improvisers use the jazz melodic minor scale to construct melodies and solo riffs in a wide range of minor contexts. Here is a D jazz melodic minor scale based on the Aeolian mode of major-scale fingering Type 4. Compare this pattern with the harmonic minor scale in the previous section. Then try adapting other Aeolian fingering patterns to play jazz melodic minor scales in other keys and positions.

Lydian Flat-Seven Scales

You are already familiar with the Lydian scale, which is built on the fourth degree of the major scale. The *Lydian flat-seven scale* is a useful variation commonly heard in jazz music. As its name implies, this scale is formed by lowering the 7th degree of the Lydian scale. (It may also be viewed as the "Lydian mode" of the jazz melodic minor scale, discussed in the previous section.)

Jazz players often use the Lydian flat-seven scale when soloing over dominant seventh chords (although they often switch to the related Mixolydian scale over V7—the true dominant seventh chord). Now try playing this Lydian flat-seven scale pattern using major-scale fingering Type 4 (with a raised 4th and lowered 7th). Then try adapting other major-scale fingering types to play Lydian flat-seven scales in different keys and positions.

Open-String Scales

Open strings create deep, natural-sounding tones which show off the guitar's resonant quality to its full advantage. For this reason, guitarists sometimes choose open-string scale forms, particularly for arrangements that call for a powerful and resonant sound.

By nature, open-string scales are not moveable. The scales that can be played in this way are limited by the fixed pitches of the instrument's open strings. Because of this limitation, there are comparatively few practical open-string scale patterns.

Since the fingerings for open-string scales are a bit more difficult than the usual positions, it really pays to practice them. If you play fingerstyle, you should have no trouble following the fingering indications (*p*=thumb, *i*=index, *m*=middle, *a*=ring). Pick-style players should use alternating pick and fingers, as shown.

Below are several typical open-string patterns for scales you have learned in previous sections of this book. Practice these examples, and then try coming up with your own open-string patterns.

Remember that the major and pentatonic scale fingerings may also be applied to the modes of the keys in which they are shown. For example, the D major pattern may also be used for an A Mixolydian or E Dorian scale—and the G major pentatonic fingering may be used for an E minor pentatonic blues scale.

D Major Open-String Scale

G Major Pentatonic Open-String Scale

Tap-On Scales

A *tap-on* is basically a hammeron that is played with a finger of the picking hand. Most guitarists use the middle finger for tapping (indicated by a *T*). A tap-on is usually followed by a pulloff to the note below. This tap-on/pulloff sequence is then followed by another pulloff performed by the fretting hand. The resulting three-note pattern gives a triplet feel to tap-on riffs and scales. If you are interested in mastering this interesting technique, it really pays to practice scales that incorporate tap-ons in sequence. Below are two typical tap-on patterns for scales you have learned in previous sections of this book. Practice these examples, and then try coming up with your own tap-on patterns.

E Aeolian Open-String Scale

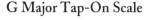

G Major Tap-On Scale

A Minor Pentatonic Open-String Scale

G Harmonic Minor Tap-On Scale

G Whole-Tone Open-String Scale

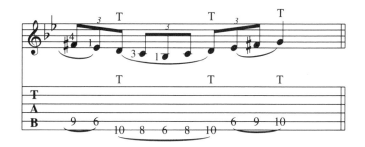

Scales Using Harmonics

Harmonics are often used in a solo context to evoke a haunting or introspective quality. Here is a G major pentatonic scale which will help you build your harmonic chops. This scale uses all natural harmonics played at the twelfth fret.

G Major Pentatonic Scale With Harmonics

You can play this scale in other keys by barring at any fret and using *artificial harmonics*. To play an artificial harmonic, lightly touch the string with the tip of the extended index finger of your picking hand at the point twelve frets above the fretted note. Then pluck the string with your thumb to sound the octave harmonic. Here are three more scales using artificial harmonics.

D Minor Pentatonic Scale With Harmonics

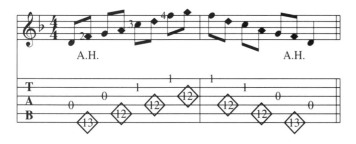

E Semitonal Pentatonic Scale With Harmonics

C Major Scale With Harmonics

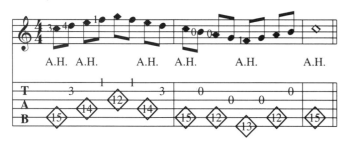

Ethnic Scales

Many contemporary guitarists and composers have found inspiration by exploring the scales of other cultures, particularly those of the Eastern Hemisphere. You have already learned many important ethnic scales in previous sections of this book. For instance, tonal and semitonal pentatonic scales are found in the music of diverse ancient and modern cultures, from the native tribes of America and Africa to Indonesia and the Far East.

In this section, you will find additional ethnic scales which feature interesting "non-diatonic" harmonies. Certain of these scales traditionally feature microtonal harmonies which have here been interpreted for use with the standard guitar tuning. Although these scales may sound inappropriate in traditional settings, they can be very effective in contemporary new age and "world" music contexts.

Gypsy Minor Scale

The *Gypsy minor scale* (also called *Hungarian minor*) features a lowered 3rd and 6th, and a raised 4th. It may also be viewed as a harmonic minor scale with a raised 4th. This distinctive scale is common in the folk music of Eastern Europe and occurs in contemporary Turkish and Jewish music as well. During the 19th and 20th centuries, Béla Bartók and other composers devoted much attention to this interesting scale and its applications in contemporary classical music.

Neapolitan Minor Scale

The *Neapolitan minor scale* features a lowered 2nd, 3rd, and 6th degree—and may also be viewed as a harmonic minor scale with a lowered 2nd. This scale is identified with the *Neapolitan School*, a term loosely applied to an Italian style of composition popular in the 18th century.

Japanese Scales

Hirajoshi Scale

Kumoi Scale

In Scale

African Scales

Tanzanian Scale

Congolese Scale

Indian Scales

Bhairava Scale

Pooravi Scale

Marava Scale

Kanakangi Scale

Balinese Scale

Pelog Scale

 # Book 4

Guitar Chord Dictionary

The versatile guitarist knows how chords are constructed—and can play a given chord in several different ways. Your choice of chord voicings is key to creating the style of music you want to play. Open tunings provide another palette of interesting sounds that can make your guitar playing sound down-home, foreign, or even otherworldly. In this book, you can learn how chords are built and named as well as how they are played in a variety of tunings.

Basic Chord Theory

This section provides an introduction to basic chord construction. Here you will find the blueprints for many common guitar chords, with corresponding diagrams and symbols.

Section Contents

Major Chords and Inversions

Three notes played simultaneously produce a *triad*, which is the simplest form of chord. (Two notes sound together would be designated as an *interval*.) Understanding and playing the basic chords that follow will help to deepen your understanding of music as well as develop your musical ear.

Reading a Chord Diagram

Chord diagrams, also called *chord boxes, chord windows,* or *chord frames,* make it easy to learn new chords. You will often see chord diagrams above the melody line in songbooks. A chord diagram shows you where to put your left-hand fingers on the strings of the guitar—and tells you the name of the chord you are playing.

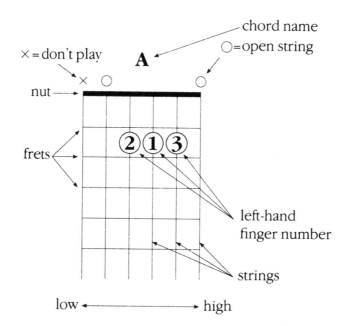

Major Chord

Let's take a look at some basic chord forms based on the note C. The *C major triad,* or *C major chord,* is formed by taking the first (or *root*), third, and fifth degrees of the C major scale. The abbreviation for this chord—its *chord symbol*—is *C.*

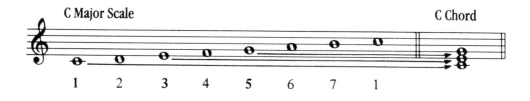

Inversions

When the lowest note of a chord is not the root, the chord is called an *inversion*. The note that is on the bottom is said to be "in the bass." When the third is in the bass, the chord is said to be "in first inversion."

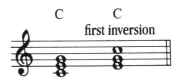

When the fifth is in the bass, the chord is said to be "in second inversion."

Sometimes a chord symbol will indicate what note is to be placed in the bass. This is done by separating the chord name and the name of the bass note with a slash. Thus, "C, first inversion" becomes "C/E" and "C, second inversion" becomes "C/G."

Seventh Chord

A *C7 chord* (pronounced "C seven") is formed by simply adding a flatted seventh to the C triad.

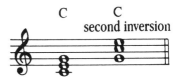

Here are several ways to play the C7 chord, including a few inversions.

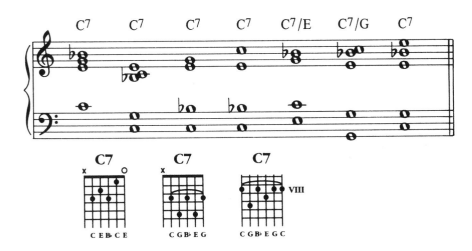

Minor and Embellished Chords

Major, minor, augmented, and *diminished* are terms that describe the *quality* of a chord. When additional tones are added to a triad, they are called *embellishments.* The basic embellishments for major and minor chords are sevenths and sixths.

Minor Chord

If you lower the third of a C major chord by one half-step, you get a *C minor chord.* The C minor chord is abbreviated *Cm.*

As with any chord, there are many ways to play Cm. Here are a few good voicings.

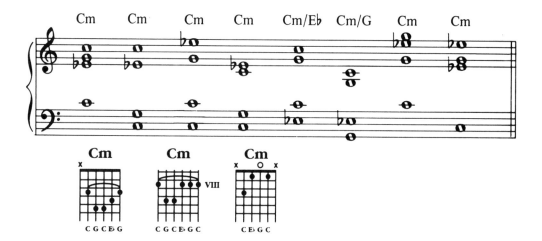

Minor Seventh Chord

Add the flatted seventh to the C minor chord and the *C minor seventh chord* results. This chord is abbreviated *Cm7.*

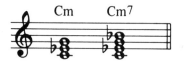

Try playing these forms of the C minor seventh chord.

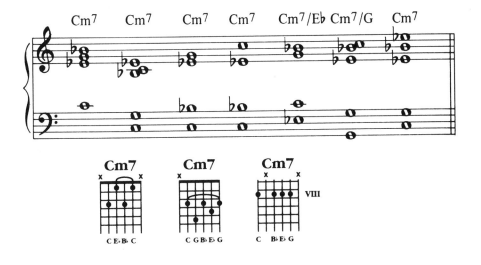

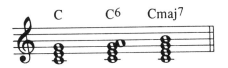

Augmented and Diminished Chords

An *augmented chord* is a major triad with a sharped fifth. The abbreviation for an augmented chord is a plus sign (+) or *aug.* A *diminished chord* is formed by flatting the fifth of a minor chord and is abbreviated with the degree sign (°) or *dim.*

Diminished chords are usually embellished by the addition of the double-flatted seventh (°7).

Major Sixth and Major Seventh Chords

Major sixth and *major seventh chords* are often used in place of regular major chords. They are formed by adding the sixth or seventh degree, respectively, to a major triad. The symbol for a major sixth chord is simply the numeral *6.* A major seventh chord is indicated by the symbol *maj7* or *M7.*

Table of Chord Symbols

Here is a list of chord-types, together with the abbreviations found in common use. The chords based on C are given as an example, but the equivalent relationships apply in all keys.

C (C △)	C major C-E-G
CM7 (C Maj 7, C△7, C7)	C major seventh C-E-G-B
CM9 (C Maj 9, C△9)	C major ninth C-E-G-B-D
C6	C (major) sixth C-E-G-A
C6/9 (C9/6)	C sixth, add ninth C-E-G-D-A
Cm (Cmin, C-)	C minor C-E♭-G
Cm7 (Cmin7, C-7)	C minor seventh C-E♭-G-B♭
Cm6 (Cmin6, C-6)	C minor sixth C-E♭-G-A
Cm9 (Cmin9, C-9)	C minor ninth C-E♭-G-B♭-D
Cm7♭5 (Cmin7♭5, C-7-5, Cø)	C minor seventh flat fifth C-E♭-G♭-B♭
C7	C seventh, (C dominant seventh) C-E-G-B♭
C7sus4	C seventh suspended fourth C-F-G-B♭
C9	C ninth (C dominant ninth) C-E-G-B♭-D
C7♭5 (C7-5)	C seventh flat fifth C-E-G♭-B♭
C7♭9 (C7-9)	C seventh flat ninth C-E-G-B♭-D♭
C7♯9 (C7+9)	C seventh sharp ninth C-E-G-B♭-D♯
C11	for practical purposes = C7sus4
C13	C thirteenth C-E-G-B♭-(D)-A
Co (Cdim, C-)	C diminished C-E♭-G♭. For practical purposes, this chord does not exist in folk, pop, and jazz music. When you see this symbol, it is shorthand for C°7.
C°7 (Cdim7, C-7)	C diminished seventh. C-E♭-G♭-B♭♭ (=C-E♭-G♭-A)
C+ (Caug)	C augmented C-E-G♯
C+7 (C7+, Caug7)	C augmented seventh, C seventh augmented C-E-G♯-B♭

Be careful to note that different editors and arrangers might use the minus sign (-) to mean either minor or diminished. Your own best bet to avoid confusion is to use one of the other abbreviations instead. If you're learning a song and don't know what the editor means, try minor first, since minor chords are more common. But you might have to try both minor and diminished to see which sounds right.

Chords in Standard Tuning

The chords in the following section are arranged according to the chromatic scale:

C   C♯/D♭   D   D♯/E♭   E   F   F♯/G♭   G   G♯/A♭   A   A♯/B♭   B

Several different positions are provided for each quality (major, minor, *etc.*) and alteration (seventh, ninth, *etc.*). This gives you a choice of where on the neck to play the particular chord and/or how the notes of the chord are arranged.

Section Contents

Standard Guitar Chords

C Chords

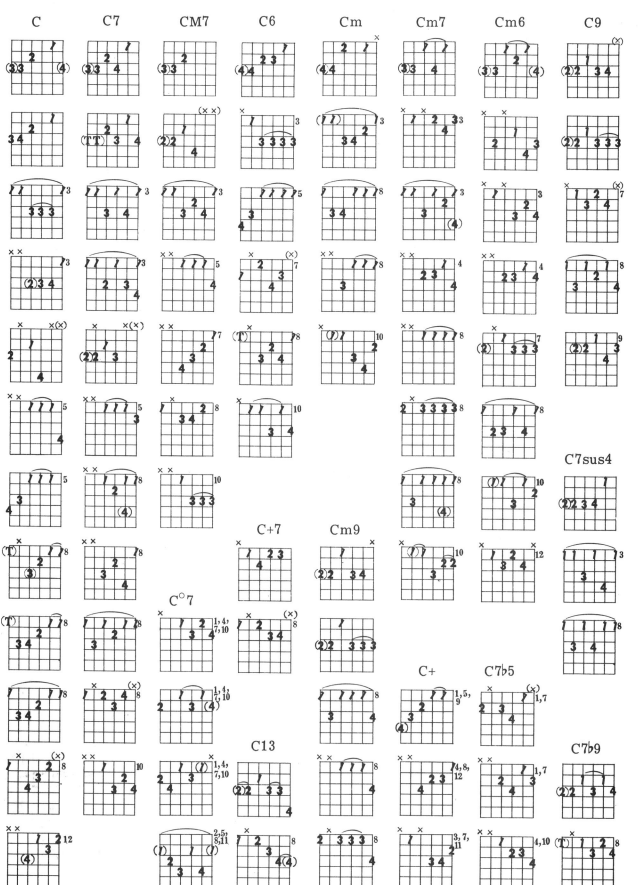

C#/Db Chords

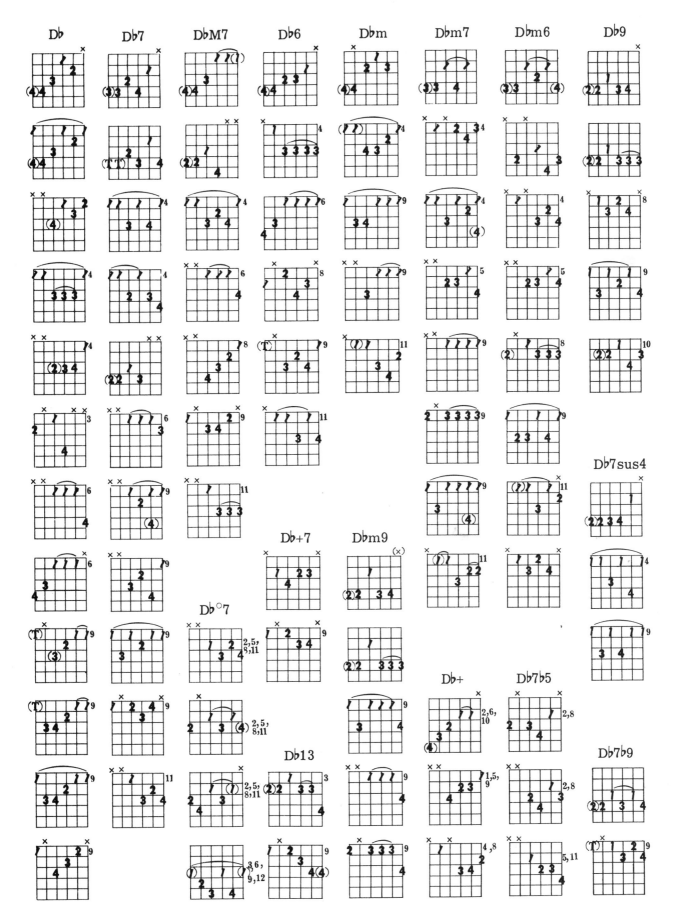

D Chords

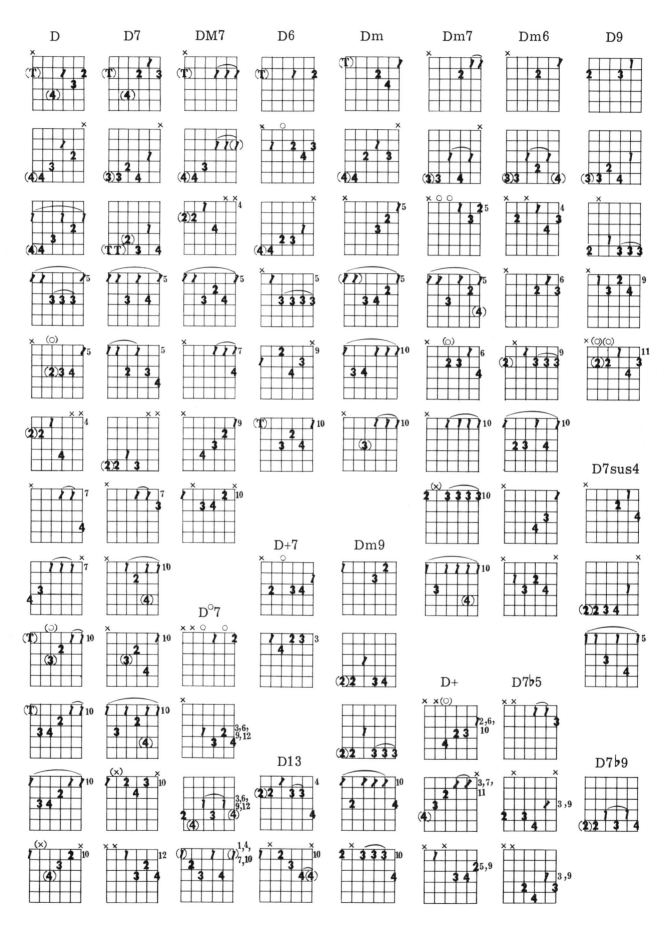

D#/Eb Chords

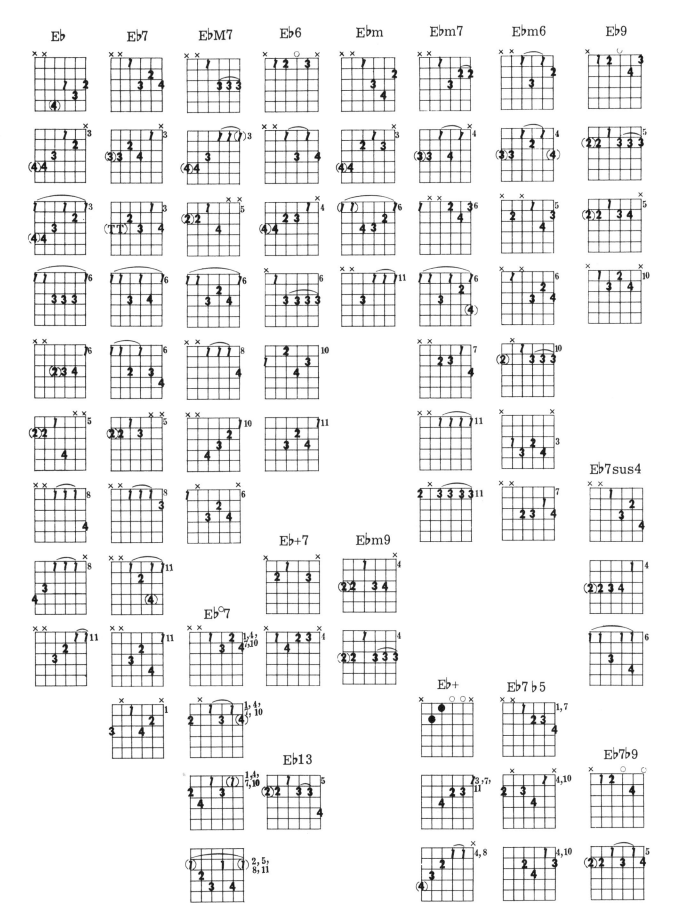

E Chords

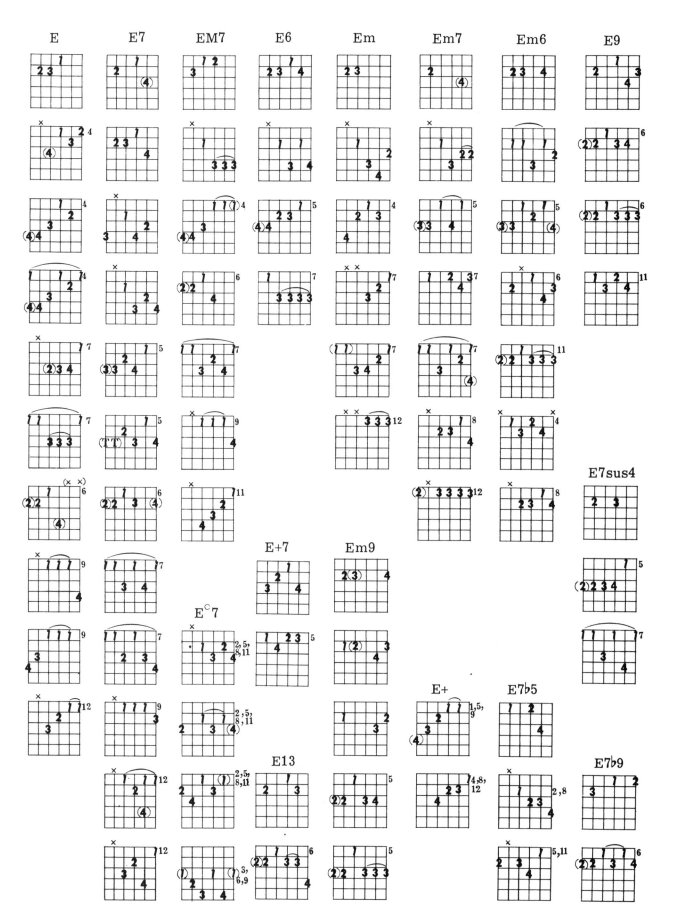

F Chords

F♯/G♭ Chords

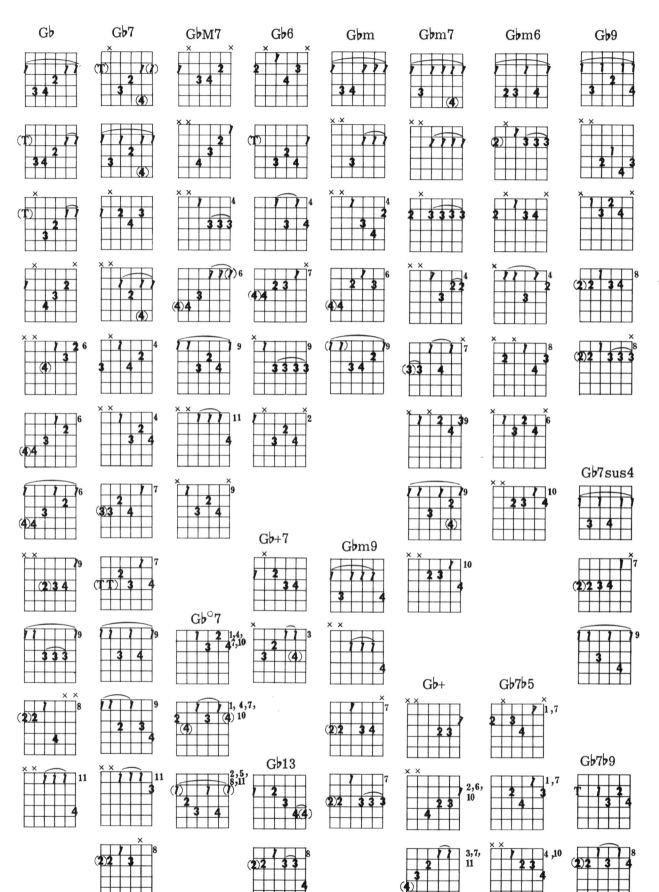

G Chords

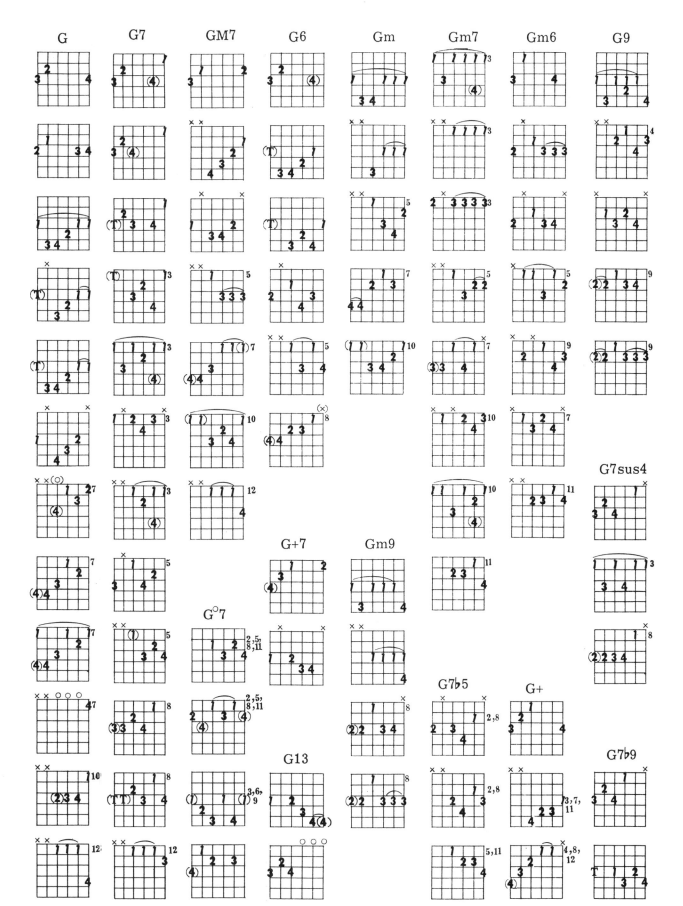

G♯/A♭ Chords

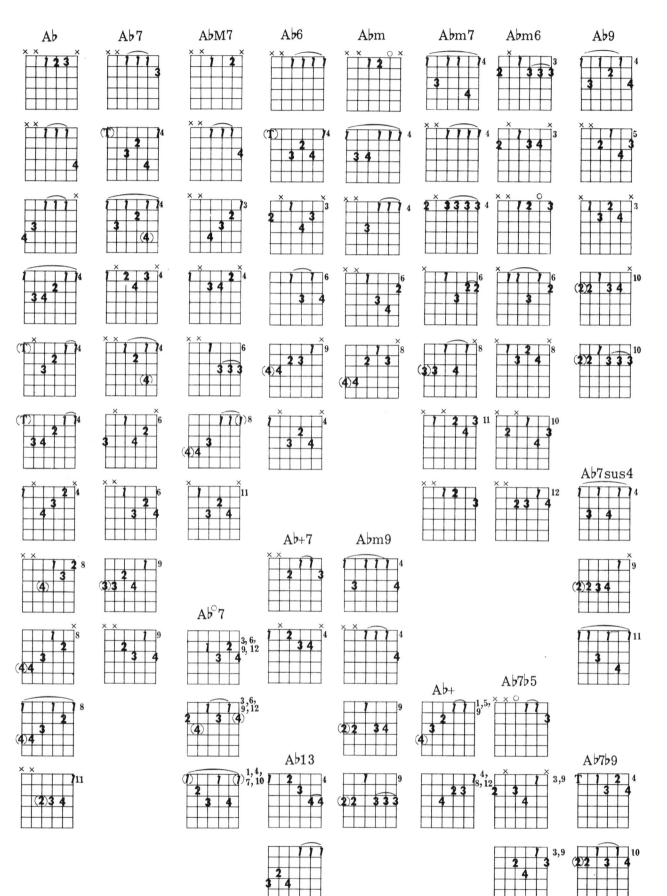

A Chords

A♯/B♭ Chords

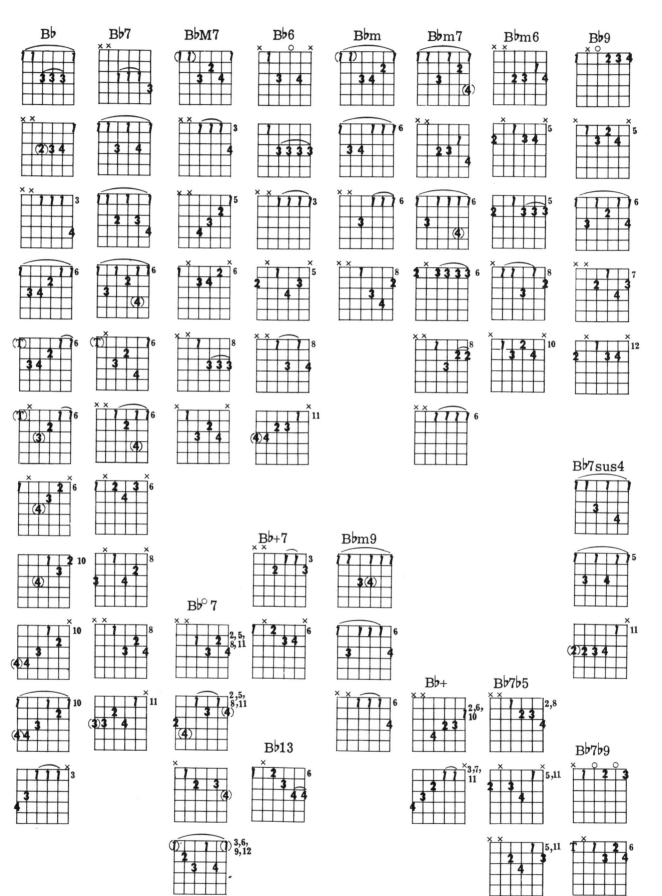

B Chords

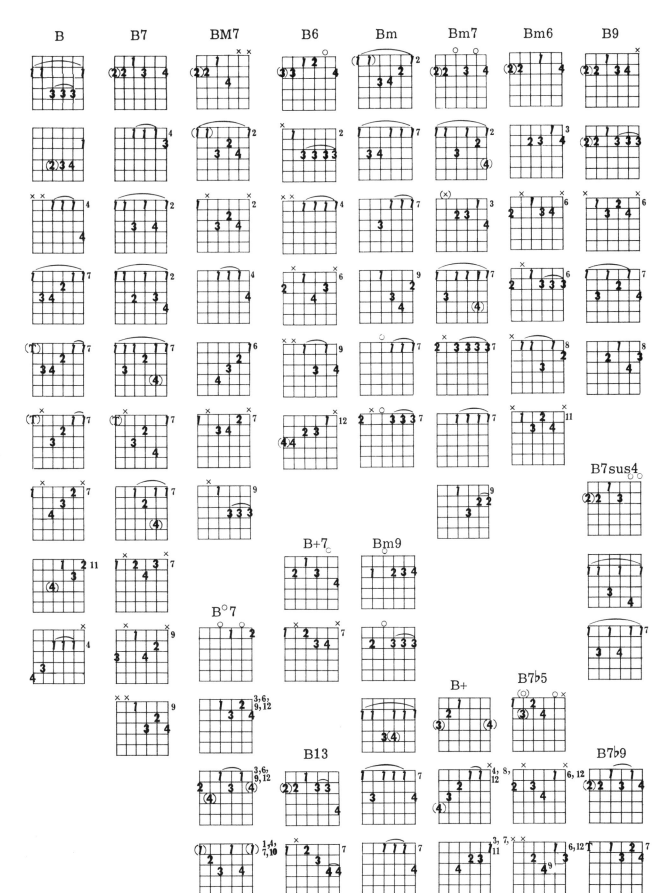

Chords in Open Tunings

The "standard" way of tuning a guitar—EADGBE—wasn't always the standard. This method evolved over hundreds of years, with input from several different cultures. However, many styles of ethnic and historic music are characterized by non-standard tunings. Alternate tunings also provide the contemporary guitarist with a rich palette of new sounds and effects. The sections that follow will give you a taste of the more common open tunings available to the guitarist, along with a selection of chord forms in each tuning.

Section Contents

Open G Tuning (DGDGBD)

In this tuning the guitar is tuned to an open G chord:

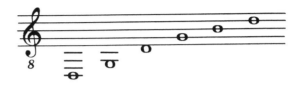

This versatile tuning corresponds to G tuning on the banjo. Occasionally it is used as an A tuning, with each string tuned one tone higher so that an open A chord results. In this case, the chords in the following diagrams should be named one tone higher (G becomes A, C7 becomes D7, etc.).

People often call this tuning "Spanish" tuning.

Chords in Open G Tuning

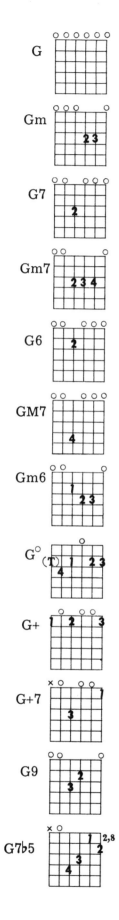
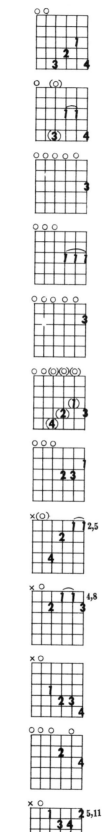
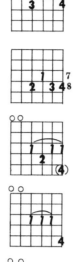

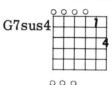

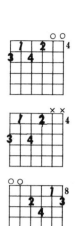

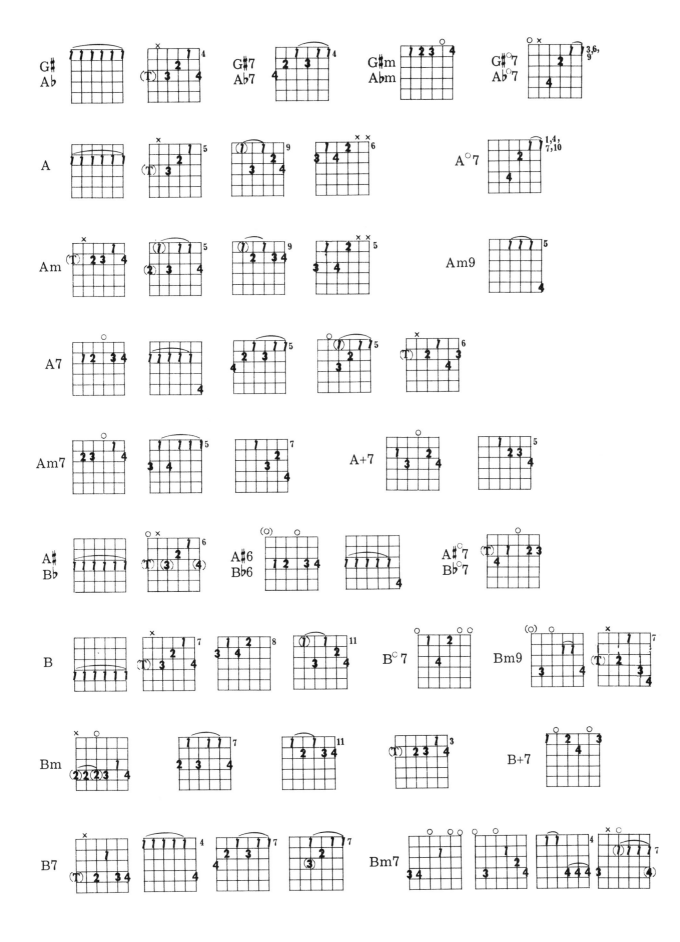

Chords in Open G Tuning

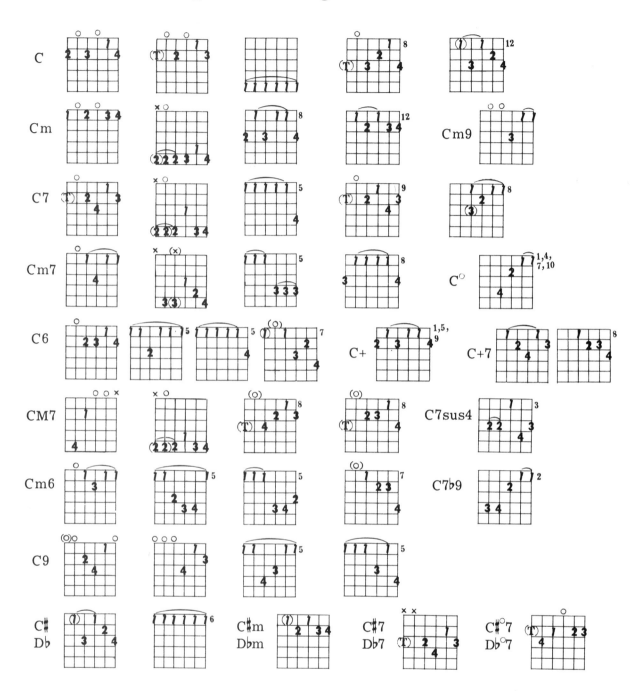

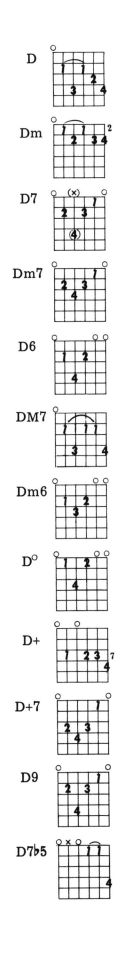

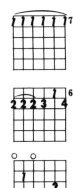

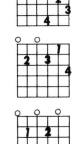

Chords in Open G Tuning

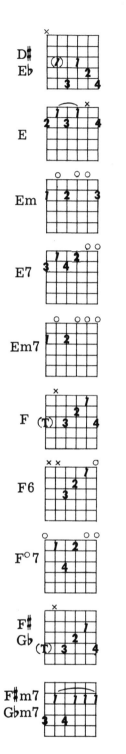

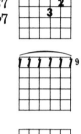

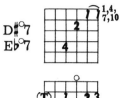

Open D Tuning (DADF#AD)

This is also known as "slack key", "Hawaiian", and "Vastopol" tuning, the last after a parlor guitar piece called "Sevastopol" that was popular in the early part of this century. The guitar is tuned to an open D major chord:

Open D is probably the most versatile of tunings, lending itself to just about any sort of song in any style, including slide and lap-steel styles.

Some players prefer to tune their instruments to an open E chord (EBEG#BE) with each string one tone higher than in D tuning. This produces a brighter sound, since the strings are tighter, but it may be rough on your strings and on the neck of your guitar. If you use E instead of D, name the chords on the diagrams that follow one tone higher (e.g. D becomes E, A7 becomes B7, etc.)

Chords in Open D Tuning

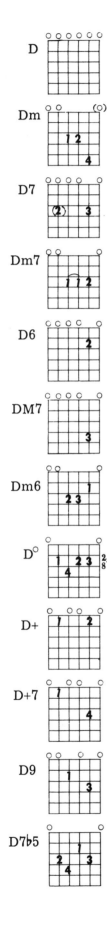

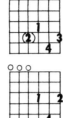

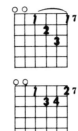

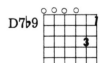

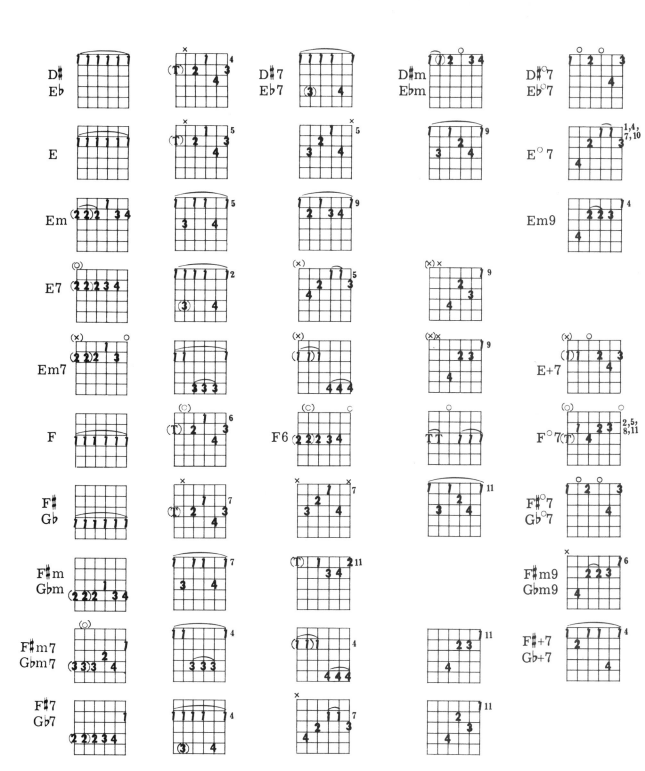

Chords in Open D Tuning

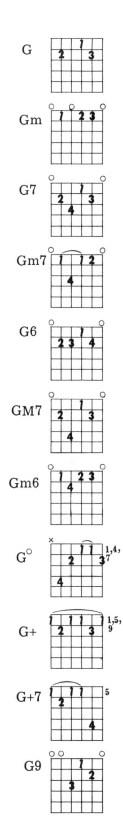

G

Gm

G7

Gm7

G6

GM7

Gm6

G°

Gm9

G+

G7
sus4

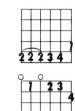

G+7

G7♭9

G9

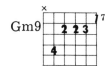

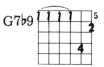

G♯
A♭

G♯7
A♭7

G♯m
A♭m

G♯°7
A♭°7

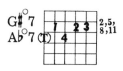

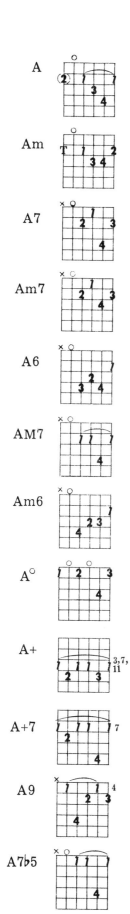

A

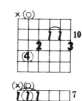

Am

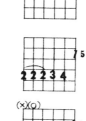

A7

Am7

A6

AM7

Am6

A°

A+

Am9

A7
sus4

A+7

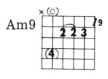

A7♭9

A9

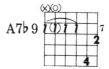

A7♭5

Chords in Open D Tuning

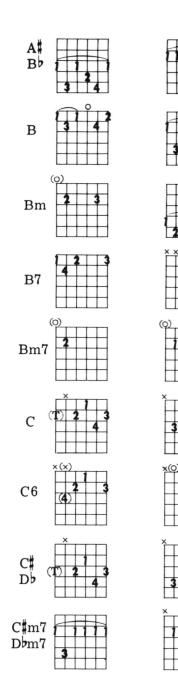

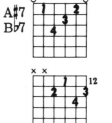

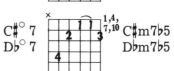

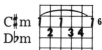

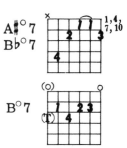

D Modal Tuning (DADGAD)

In this tuning the guitar is tuned to a D chord with a suspended fourth and without a third. The resulting sound is not quite definable as either minor or major, and it provides a striking texture at once very modern and very archaic. This tuning is rarely used by traditional guitarists, but is favored by modern guitarists especially for bluesy sounds with very simple chord changes.

D A D G A D

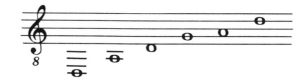

Chords in D Modal Tuning

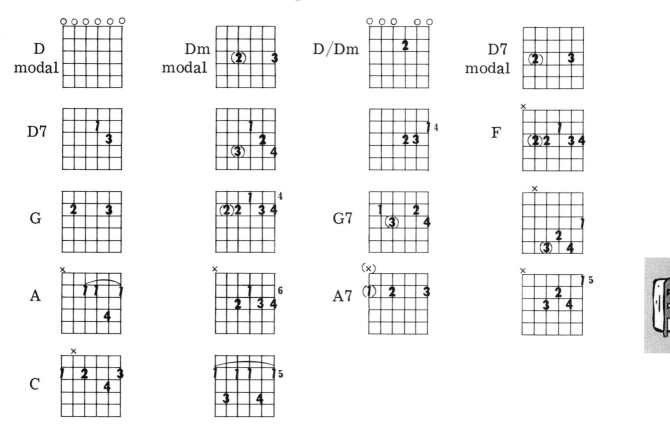

Dropped D Tuning (DADGBE)

D A D G B E

This is the same as standard tuning, with the sixth string dropped one whole tone to D in order to facilitate playing in the key of D, particularly in fingerpicking style where an alternating bass note pattern is called for. You can use any chord shape from standard tuning as long as you leave out the sixth string. In addition, you can work out new fingerings by compensating for the two-fret drop of the sixth string. The fingerings below are in common use:

Chords in Dropped D Tuning

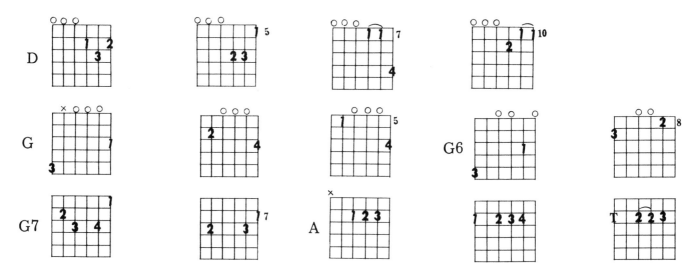

D Minor "Crossnote" Tuning (DADFAD)

The guitar is tuned to an open D minor chord, but the actual playing can be done in either D minor or D major.

D A D F A D

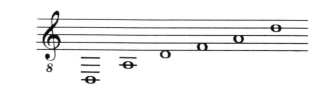

This tuning is called "cross-note" (or sometimes "cross-key") because the old-time bluesmen found it so effective for crossing over between minor and major tonalities. It also serves admirably as a vehicle for minor key songs that don't have the remotest blues feeling about them, and some strikingly modern sounds can be had this way.

Some guitarists (especially the old bluesmen) prefer to tune the strings one tone higher to an open E minor chord: EBEGBE. This might be a bit rough on your strings and neck, but it's much easier to get in and out of the tuning this way, since only the fifth and fourth strings need to be changed from standard tuning.

Chords in D Minor Tuning

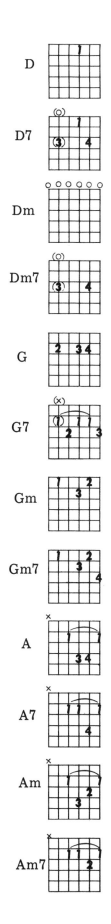
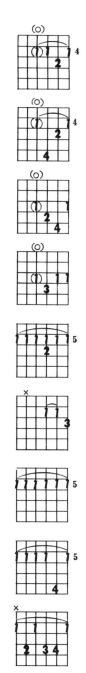
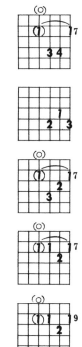

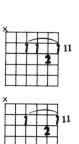

Open A Tuning (EAC♯EAE)

In this tuning, especially useful for a delta blues sound, the guitar is tuned to an open A chord:

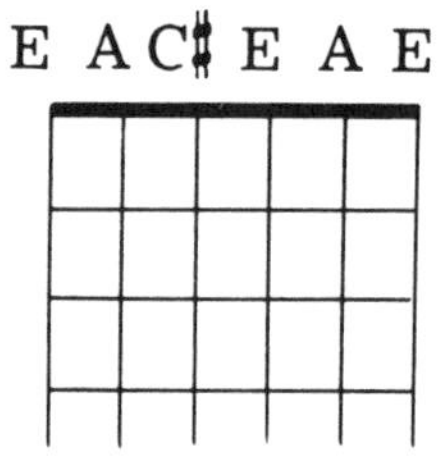

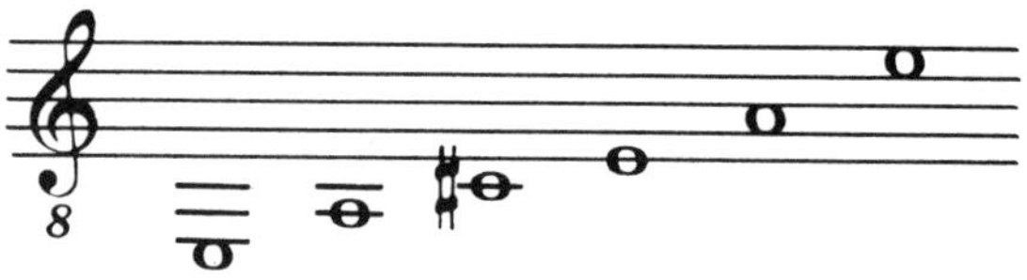

Chords in Open A Tuning

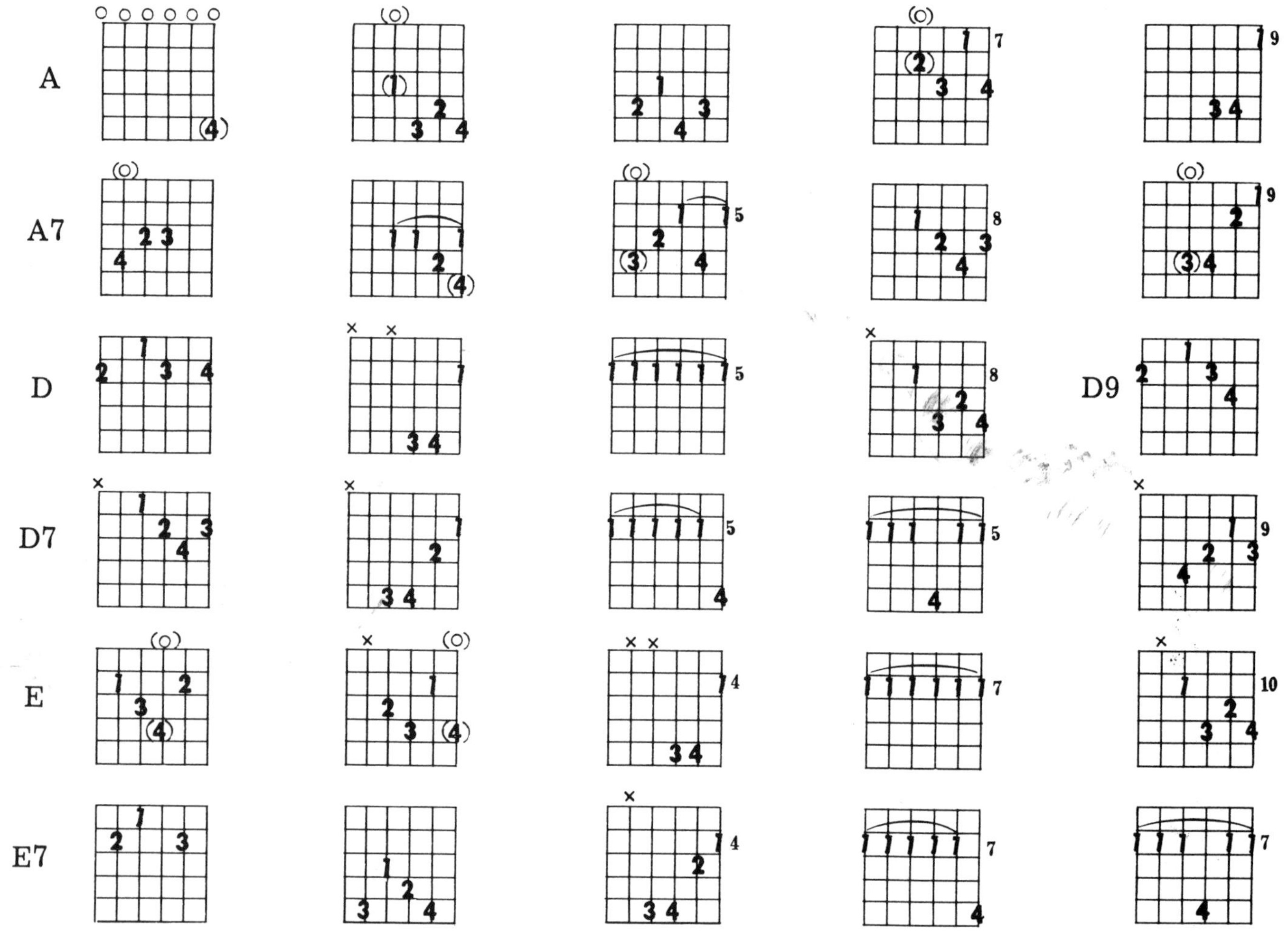

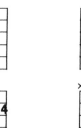

1 2 3 4 5 6 7

8 9 0

1 2 3 4 5 6 7

8 9 0

1 2

Zach

Open C Tuning (CGCGCE)

A very beautiful tuning not used today as often as formerly. This is surprising, since it represents possibilities for a whole array of sounds from the funkiest of blues to the laciest of filigree ballad accompaniments, from the most archaic to the most modern of sounds. A few of the old-timers I've met use this tuning for pieces that are mostly played today in G and D tunings. The guitar is tuned to an open C chord, corresponding to open C tuning on the banjo:

C G C G C E

Chords in Open C Tuning

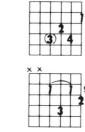

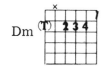

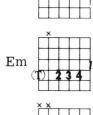
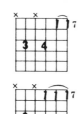

Chords in Open C Tuning

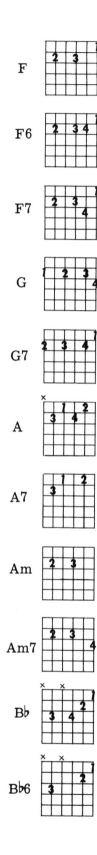
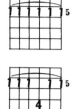

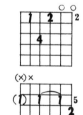

Book 5

Guitarist's Guide to Other Fretted Instruments

Most guitarists can pick up any fretted instrument and get some sort of sound out of it without too much effort. That's because the basic playing methods for all fretted instruments are pretty much the same. What differs is the idiomatic tunings, playing styles, and techniques peculiar to each instrument.

In this book, you will find information on the tuning and basic chord forms for specialty guitars and other fretted instruments. These include most of the instruments guitarists find useful as a second instrument in a variety of musical styles. Some of these fretted instruments are very similar to the guitar—and a few are even tuned the same as the guitar. Others require their own special tunings and chord forms. With time and practice, you should be able to master any of these fretted instruments. The chords and tunings provided here should give you an excellent start.

Contents   Page

Twelve-String Guitar, Ukulele, Baritone Ukulele, and Tenor Guitar

The instruments covered in this section are closely related to the guitar because they are tuned in a similar way. Here you will find tuning instructions for each of these guitar-related instruments. There is also information on how to easily adapt the standard guitar chord diagrams, which are found in the section entitled "Chords in Standard Tuning" in *Book 4: Guitar Chord Dictionary.*

Section Contents

Twelve-String Guitar

The twelve-string guitar has a full, rich sound that can be heard in many popular venues. This type of guitar has six pairs of strings—and each pair is called a *course*. Each course is picked and fretted as if it were one string.

To understand how the twelve-string guitar is tuned, first take a look at the tuning for the standard six string guitar.

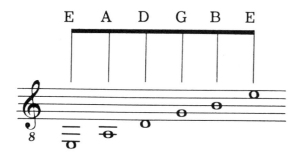

The twelve-string guitar is essentially a six-string guitar with doubled strings. The lower courses are tuned in octaves. The strings in each of the two highest courses are tuned to the same pitch (in unison).

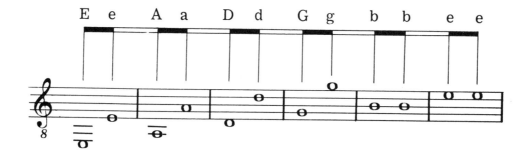

Because the twelve-string guitar is tuned to the same pitches as the six-string guitar, you can use all the chords found in the section "Chords in Standard Tuning" in *Book 4: Guitar Chord Dictionary.* Although most newer twelve-string guitars may be tuned up to pitch, many guitarists prefer to keep their instruments tuned one whole step (two frets) lower, that is: DD GG CC FF AA DD. If you do this, you should put a capo on the second fret to play standard guitar chords at pitch.

Ukulele and Baritone Ukulele

The ukulele is also closely related to the guitar because it is tuned in a similar way. The baritone ukulele is tuned to the exact same pitches as the top four strings of the guitar. This makes it very easy for a guitarist to pick up the baritone uke. Just disregard the bottom two strings of the chord diagrams found in "Chords in Standard Tuning" in *Book 4: Guitar Chord Dictionary.*

The top three strings of the ukulele are tuned a fifth higher than the top three strings of the guitar. The fourth string of the ukulele is tuned one octave and a fifth higher than the fourth string of the guitar.

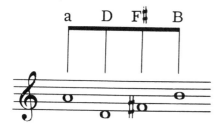

This means that you can adapt all the chords found in the section "Chords in Standard Tuning" in *Book 4: Guitar Chord Dictionary.* Just choose the chord that is a fifth lower than the one you wish to play, and disregard the bottom two strings of the chord diagram.

Guitar		Ukulele
C	=	G
C♯/D♭	=	G♯/A♭
D	=	A
D♯/E♭	=	A♯/B♭
E	=	B
F	=	C
F♯/G♭	=	C♯/D♭
G	=	D
G♯/A♭	=	D♯/E♭
A	=	E
A♯/B♭	=	F
B	=	F♯/G♭

Tenor Guitar

There are three common ways to tune the tenor guitar. First, it may be tuned like the first four strings of the guitar, but a fourth higher.

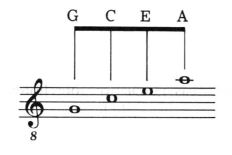

In this tuning, you can adapt all the chords found in the section "Chords in Standard Tuning" in **Book 4: Guitar Chord Dictionary.** Just choose the chord that is a fourth lower than the one you wish to play, and disregard the bottom two strings of the chord diagram.

Guitar		Tenor Guitar
C	=	F
C♯/D♭	=	F♯/G♭
D	=	G
D♯/E♭	=	G♯/A♭
E	=	A
F	=	A♯/B♭
F♯/G♭	=	B
G	=	C
G♯/A♭	=	C♯/D♭
A	=	D
A♯/B♭	=	D♯/E♭
B	=	E

The tenor guitar may also be tuned a fifth higher than the standard guitar. In this tuning, you can adapt all the chords found in the section "Chords in Standard Tuning" in **Book 4: Guitar Chord Dictionary.** Just choose the chord that is a fifth lower than the one you wish to play, and disregard the bottom two strings of the chord diagram (see the transposition chart for the ukulele on previous page).

The tenor guitar is also often tuned in fifths, the same as a tenor banjo (CGDA). For this tuning, you may use the chords found in the section "Mandolin, Mandola, Mandocello, and Tenor Banjo."

Bass Guitar

The bass guitar is a mainstay in many styles of contemporary music. The acoustic and electric bass guitars are closely related to the guitar because they are tuned in a similar way. In fact, it's easy for a guitarist to learn bass because the four strings of the bass are an octave lower than the four lowest strings of the guitar. Many guitarists find it useful to be able to double on this instrument. In this section, you will find four different tuning methods for the bass guitar.

Although full chords are not commonly played on the bass guitar, two-note chords and arpeggios are integral to many bass guitar styles. If you would like to explore playing chords on the bass, simply disregard the top two strings of any standard chord diagram. These are found in the section entitled "Chords in Standard Tuning" in *Book 4: Guitar Chord Dictionary.*

Section Contents

Tuning

Here are four ways to get in tune.

Relative Tuning

If you know that your bass is close to pitch you can use this method to make sure that it is in tune with itself:

- Fret the E, or fourth, string at the fifth fret. This note is A and should sound the same as the open A, or third, string. If the A string does not sound in tune, loosen it until it sounds lower than the fourth string, fifth fret. Slowly bring it up to pitch.

- When your A string is in tune, fret it at the fifth fret. This note is D and should sound the same as the open D, or second, string.

- When your D string is in tune, fret it at the fifth fret. This note is G and should sound the same as the open G, or first, string.

This diagram summarizes the relative tuning method:

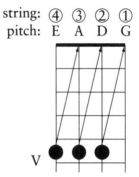

When you understand this relationship, you can use it to check any string against another. So if someone gives just one note, for instance an A, and you get one string in tune, you can tune the other three from there.

Tuning by Harmonics

Harmonics are tones produced without actually fretting a string. Instead, just touch the string lightly with a left-hand finger directly above the fret indicated. Strike (pluck) the string with your right-hand index or middle finger and remove the left-hand finger immediately. The result is a high, bell-like tone. In fact, harmonics are often referred to as 'chimes'. The easiest harmonics to sound are those produced by touching the strings at the twelfth fret. Try a few of these to get the idea before proceeding.

Like the relative tuning method above, this method can only tell you if your bass is in tune to itself. If you are playing with other people you will need to tune at least one of your strings to them before applying this method.

- Assuming that your E (fourth) string is in tune, sound the harmonic at the fifth fret. This tone (E) should sound the same as the harmonic on the A (third) string, seventh fret. If the two tones are not perfectly in unison, loosen the A string until it sounds lower and then slowly bring it up to pitch.*

- When your A string is in tune, sound its harmonic at the fifth fret. Compare and match this tone (A) to the harmonic on the D (second) string, seventh fret.

- When your D string is in tune, sound its harmonic at the fifth fret. Compare and match this tone (D) to the harmonic on the G (first) string, seventh fret.

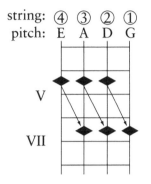

Tuning to a Guitar

Since the four bass strings are tuned to the same pitches as the four lowest guitar strings but one octave lower, it is a pretty simple matter to get in tune with a guitarist.

To make it easier to compare and match the pitch of each string, sound each of your strings as a harmonic at the twelfth fret. When you do this, your strings will sound exactly the same pitches as those of the guitar:

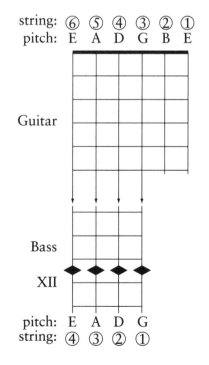

* You can see that an advantage of this method over the relative tuning method is that both tones keep ringing while you are tuning, making comparison easier.

Tuning to a Piano

Here are the notes that correspond to the open strings of the bass: *

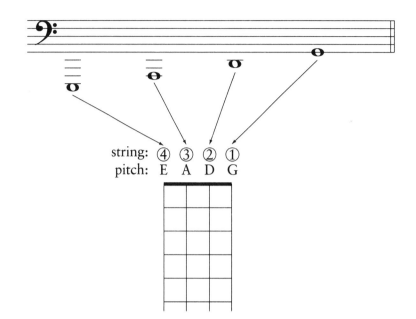

It may be easier for you to hear these tones accurately if you sound them as harmonics at the twelfth fret. This makes them sound one octave higher. Harmonics also have a purer tone, making the actual pitch more distinguishable.

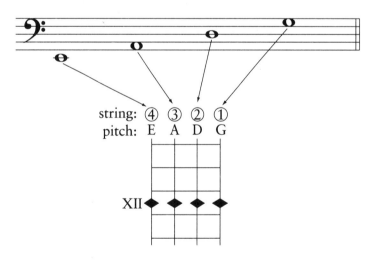

These notes represent the actual sounds of the bass strings. Music for bass is written one octave higher than it sounds to make it easier to read.

Table of Notes

In this table, the standard notation contains two sets of notes. The bass staff shows you how the notes appear when you are reading music written for the bass. This line is in *bass clef* (𝄢). The small music staff above the bass staff shows the notes in *treble clef* (𝄞) an octave above the bass-clef notes. You can use this line to help you figure out music found in songbooks, guitar books, and other sources that are not notated for bass.

Dobro and Lap Steel

This section features chords and tunings for the Dobro and lap steel, which are played with a metal *slide* or *bar*. These specialty guitars are held on the player's lap and played from above. The bar is held in the player's left hand—and fingerpicks are worn on the right hand. The lap steel and Dobro are commonly heard in folk, country, blues, bluegrass, and Hawaiian music.

The term *slide guitar* usually refers to a style of playing rather than a specific instrument. You can play slide guitar style on any steel-string guitar that has been properly set-up with a higher-than-usual action and heavy gauge strings. The *slide* is a metal or glass tube worn on the ring or pinky finger of the player's left hand. Instead of fretting, the player moves the slide up and down the strings to create the characteristic slide guitar sound.

Section Contents

Dobro

Dobro is actually a trademark name for a resophonic guitar used by the first makers of the instrument, the *Do*pera *bro*thers. It is shaped like a standard guitar but has metal resonators inside that add volume and give the instrument its distinctive tone. Many Dobros have metal bodies as well.

In standard bluegrass tuning, the Dobro is tuned to an open G chord. This is a variation of the G chord used in the open G guitar tuning.

G B D G B D

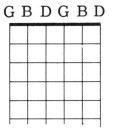
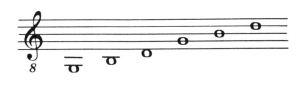

Another common tuning for the Dobro is the G Spanish tuning: DGDGBD.

Due to the limitations of playing with a bar, there are only a few full chords available for the Dobro (and lap steel). Because the Dobro is primarily a melody instrument, the use of chords is usually kept to a minimum.

The chords and partial chords shown on the following page are useful in the bluegrass tuning and Spanish tuning. Note that many of these chords require that the bar be held diagonally, which can be difficult at first. Be sure to pluck only the indicated strings (although the bar may be resting across strings that are not plucked). In different keys, many of these chord forms may be played in other positions on the neck.

The Dobro may also be tuned in open D tuning: DADF♯AD. This is an effective tuning for blues music or solo work.

In addition, there are seven- and eight-string Dobros which have several tuning possibilities with characteristic sounds.

(D)GBDGBDE for a Western swing sound

(D)GBDGBDF for a bluesy, funky sound

(D)GBEGBDF for a versatile compromise between Western swing and blues. (This tuning requires extreme care with the steel and right-hand picking.)

Lap Steel

A *lap steel* is a type of electric guitar that rests on the player's lap and is played from above, rather than being cradled in the guitarist's arms like a standard guitar. This specialty guitar is commonly heard in country, Hawaiian, and some pop and blues music. The most common tunings for the lap steel are the same as those listed above for the Dobro. Here again, the chords and partial chords on the following page are useful for the bluegrass and Spanish tunings.

Steel Positions in G

G

G6

G7

G9

G
or
Gm

Gm

C

C7

C9

C
or
Cm

D

D7

D
or
Dm

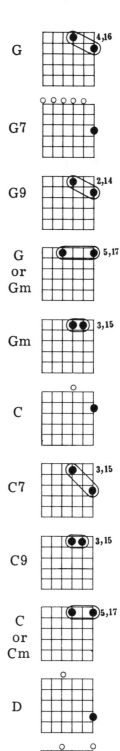

Plectrum and Five-String Banjo

The five-string and plectrum banjo are closely related. In fact, the only difference is that the plectrum banjo has four strings. The five-string banjo features an additional string which starts at the fifth fret of the neck. This adds a characteristic high drone to the overall sound.

The plectrum banjo is seldom heard in any type of contemporary music. It's use is reserved for traditional American folk, ragtime, and minstrel music, as well as 19th-century classical banjo music. As its name implies, the plectrum banjo is usually played with a pick.

The five-string banjo is commonly heard in old-time folk, bluegrass, and country music. This banjo is usually played fingerstyle in a contemporary setting. To create an old-timey feel, the player may use various techniques. These include traditional strumming (called *frailing*)—or a combination of single notes and downward strums (called *clawhammer* style).

Section Contents

Plectrum Banjo

The tuning most commonly used for this instrument is the C tuning, which is also used by the five-string banjo. Pitches and chords in this tuning are listed in the section on five-string banjo that follows.

During the 19th century, the standard tuning for the plectrum banjo was an A tuning—a minor third lower than the C tuning: AEG♯B. This lower tuning is especially suitable for old style ragtime and minstrel music.

Five-String Banjo

The five-string banjo is usually tuned to an open chord and played only in that key—or in a very few closely related keys. In order to play in keys for which a tuning does not exist, the player uses a capo or retunes all the strings a few half steps higher or lower. To change the pitch of the fifth string without retuning it, you must have a banjo with a fifth-string capo or fifth-string tuning spikes.

The high drone fifth string of this banjo is seldom fretted, so it may sometimes be dissonant with the chords that are being played. This dissonant quality gives the five-string banjo its characteristic charm. In cases where the dissonance is extreme, the fifth string should not be played.

C Tuning

The plectrum banjo almost always uses a C tuning: CGBD. The five-string banjo is also sometimes tuned in this way (with the fifth string tuned to G).

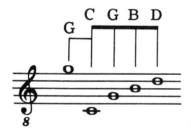

The five-string banjo rarely features this tuning in a bluegrass setting. Instead, the C tuning is used for other traditional and contemporary music, especially fiddle tunes. The C tuning works well for the keys of both C and C minor. The key of A minor (with the fifth string retuned to A) is also easily accessible. The C tuning has a very bright sound, and is especially useful for melodies that lie too low to be expressed effectively in any of the G tunings. Some tunes in C sound interesting with the fifth string retuned to E (or even D).

A few players like to retune the whole banjo one tone higher (to ADAC♯E). This is useful when accompanying fiddlers in their favorite fiddle key of D without using a capo. If you do this, be sure to pick a chord one whole step lower than the one you wish to play from the diagrams that follow. For example, if you wish to play a D chord, use a C chord from the chart.

Chords in C Tuning

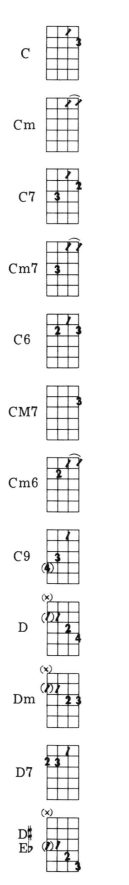

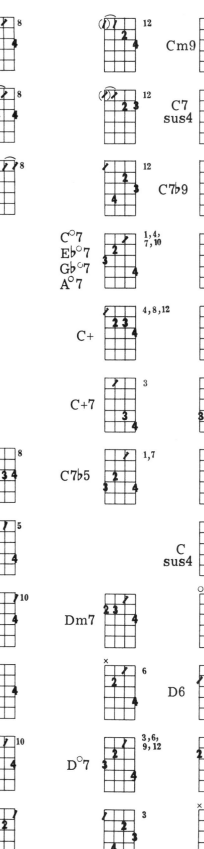

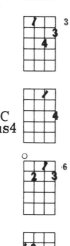

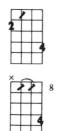

Chords in C Tuning

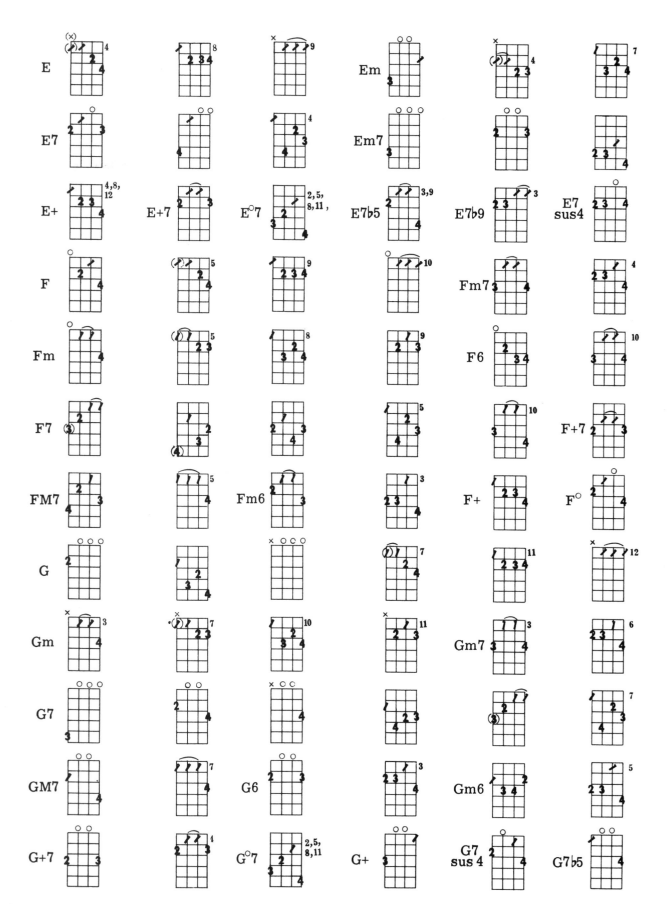

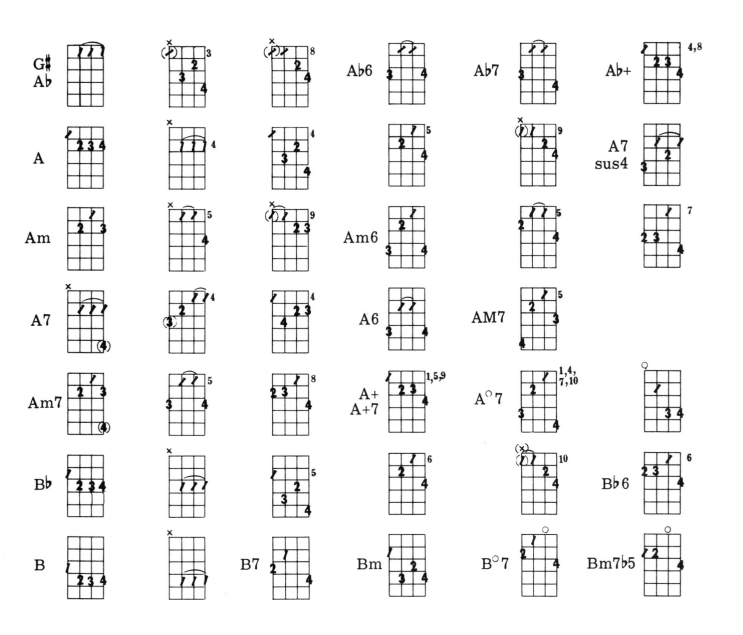

G Tuning

G tuning is the most common tuning for the five-string banjo. This is the standard tuning for bluegrass, folk, and contemporary music. Here, the banjo is tuned to an open G chord.

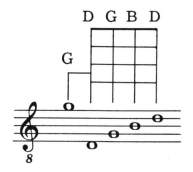

The G tuning is usually used for playing in the key of G. Of all tunings for the five-string banjo, G tuning offers the greatest potential for playing in other keys. The following keys are accessible in G tuning (with the indicated retuning or capoing of the fifth string):

A minor (with the fifth string tuned to A)

E minor (with the fifth string tuned to E)

D major (with the fifth string tuned to A or F#)

C major (with the fifth string tuned to G)

F major (with the fifth string tuned to F)

These fifth-string tuning variations can also be used to lend an exotic quality to some tunes in the key of G.

With the aid of a capo, it is possible to play the five-string banjo in any major key using G tuning. Most minor keys are also readily accessible.

Chords in G Tuning

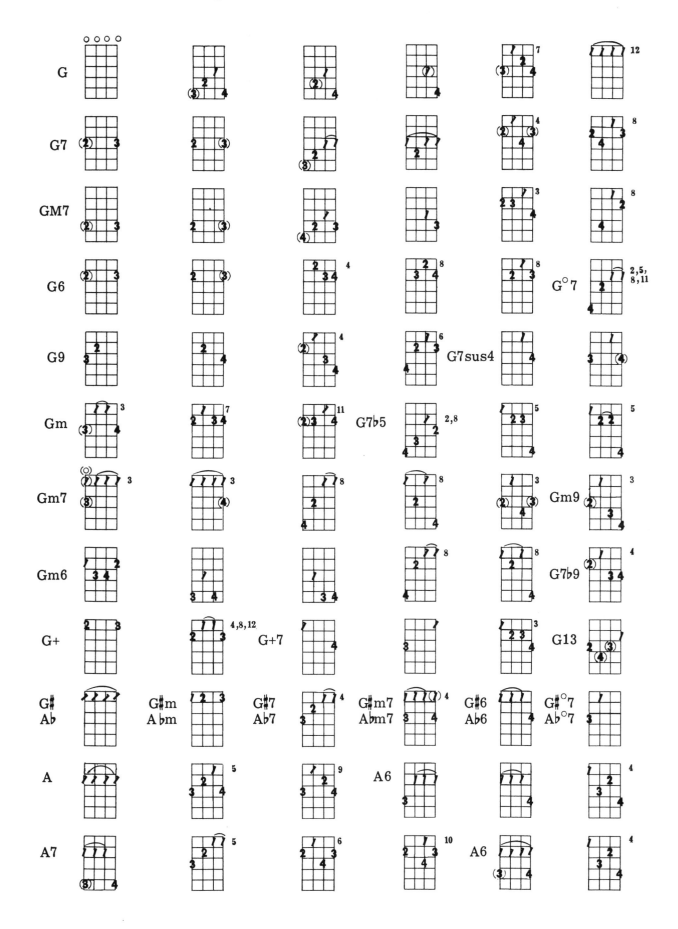

Chords in G Tuning

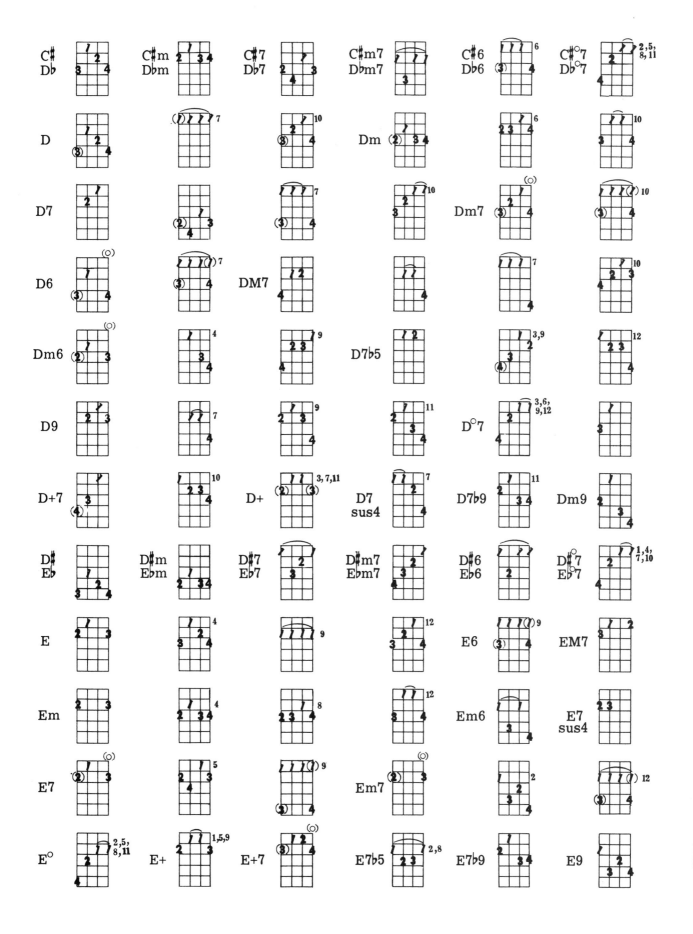

Chords in G Tuning

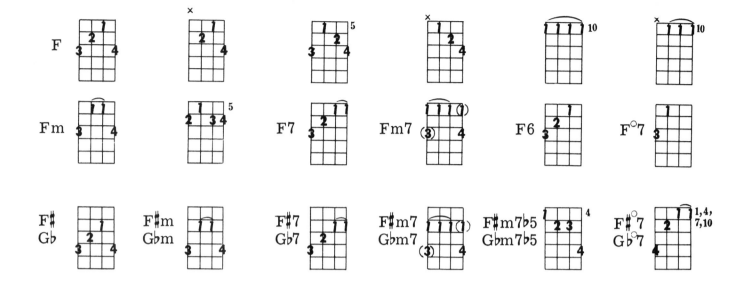

G Minor Tuning

G Minor tuning is especially effective for ballads that have a high range. It's also great for tunes where the archaic sound quality of the more frequently used G modal tuning is not desirable. It is rarely used by mountain and traditional bluegrass musicians, but it's quite common among city and newgrass musicians, especially for adapting contemporary material for the banjo.

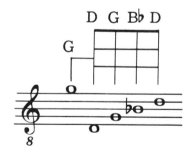

Chords in G Minor Tuning

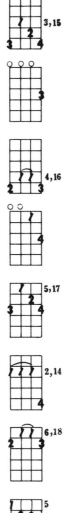

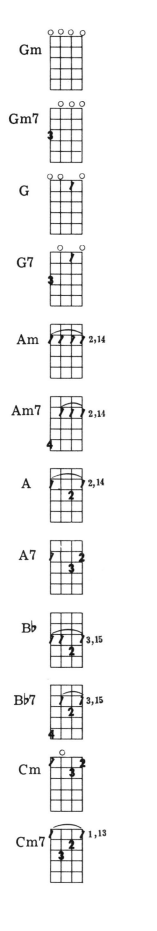

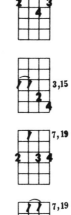

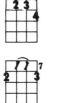

Chords in G Minor Tuning

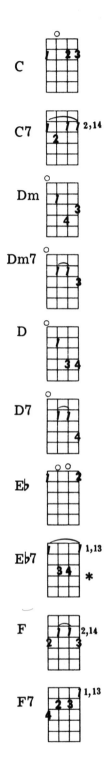
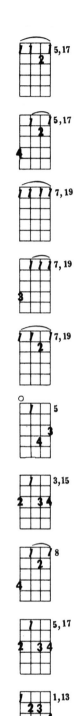
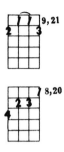

G Modal Tuning

This very beautiful and archaic sounding tuning consists of an open G chord lacking a third and with a fourth added. The resulting sound is neither major nor minor, though it would strike most people as minor because of its open, melancholy character. It is particularly useful for playing poignant melodies such as "Shady Grove," "The Cuckoo," and other old ballads. Old-time banjo players refer to this tuning variously as *sawmill tuning, mountain minor tuning,* or *'lassie-makin'* (molasses-making) *tuning.* Some players tune the fifth string down to F for certain tunes.

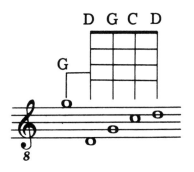

Chords in G Modal Tuning

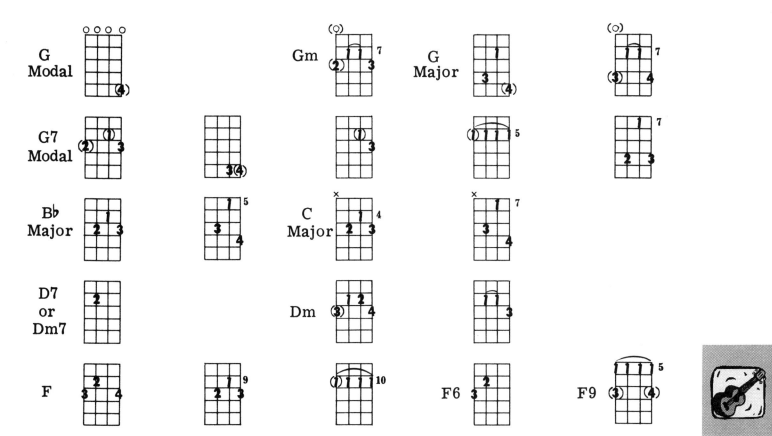

Mandolin, Mandola, Mandocello, and Tenor Banjo

The instruments of the mandolin family each have four pairs, or *courses,* of strings. The tenor banjo has four single strings. What makes all of these instruments similar is that they are all tuned in fifths and all played with a pick. They all use the same chord forms, but the various instruments sound in different keys or octaves.

In the middle to late 19th century, the mandolin was so popular that there were thousands of mandolin orchestras comprising mandolins, mandolas, mandocellos, and even mandobasses. Their repertoires ranged from popular tunes of the day to classical and operatic themes. Today the mandolin is a featured instrument in bluegrass bands and quite often in country and pop music. Mandolas and mandocellos are most often heard in Celtic and contemporary folk music.

Around the same time, the banjo enjoyed a similar popularity throughout the country. There were all sizes and types of banjos manufactured, as well as hybrid instruments such as the banjolin and banjo uke. By the 1920s and 1930s, the tenor banjo had emerged as the most practical of all of the various configurations. Of course, by the 1940s it had been almost entirely eclipsed by the popularity of the guitar.

Section Contents

Mandolin

The mandolin was designed to be a fretted and plucked counterpart to the violin. As such, it is tuned the same as a violin and has the same range.

The four courses of the mandolin are each tuned in unison: GG DD AA EE. Chords for mandolin are provided in the pages that follow.

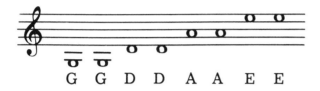

Mandola

The mandola is tuned a fifth lower than the mandolin: CC GG DD AA. The mandola uses the same tuning and chords as the tenor banjo (see below).

Mandocello

The mandocello is usually tuned an octave lower than the tenor banjo and can use the same chords (see below). The mandocello is sometimes tuned an octave below the mandolin (see the mandolin chords that follow). The mandocello may also be tuned like the first four strings of the guitar: DD GG BB EE. For this tuning, see "Chords in Standard Tuning" in *Book 4: Guitar Chord Dictionary*.

Tenor Banjo

The tenor banjo has a shorter neck than the plectrum or five-string banjo. This is the banjo heard in Dixieland and other early jazz music.

The tenor banjo is tuned a fifth lower than the mandolin: CGDA.

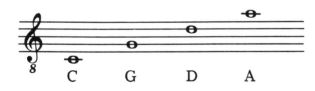

In the chord diagrams that follow, some of the chords require a stretch of an extra fret beyond the length of the diagram. These "missing" frets are indicated by the fret numbers to the right of the diagram. Most of these chords are intended only for the short fingerboard of the mandolin. A few of these are difficult or impossible to play on the longer necks of the tenor banjo, mandola, or mandocello.

Chords for Mandolin and Tenor Banjo

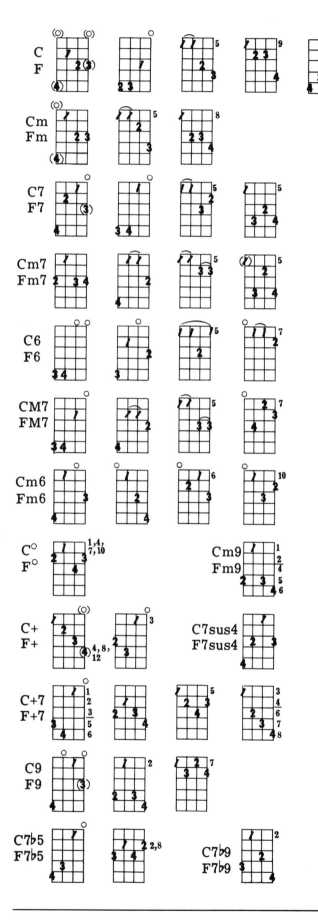

The top chord symbol next to each diagram is for the mandolin. The bottom chord symbol is for tenor banjo.

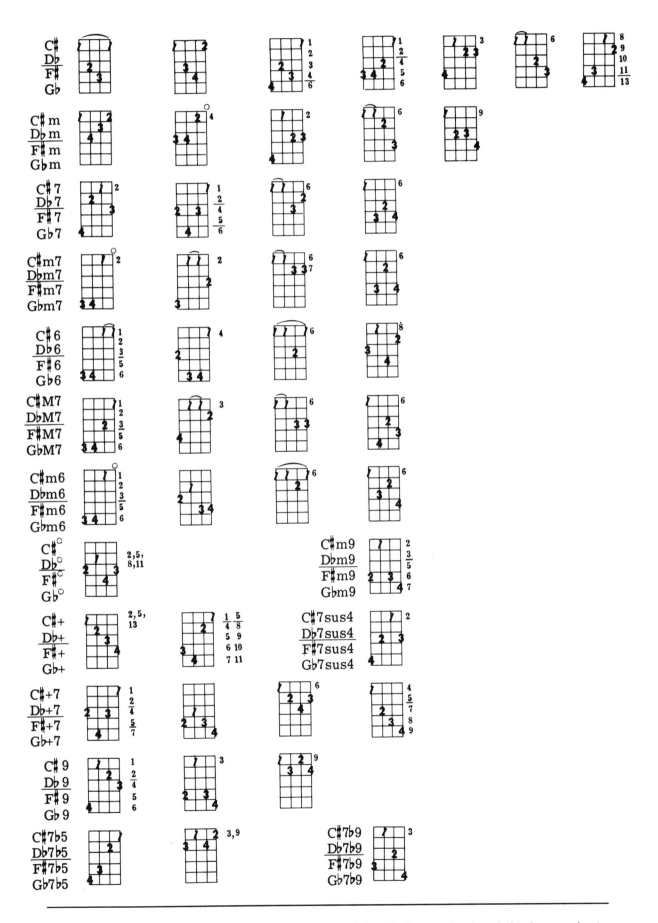

The top chord symbol next to each diagram is for the mandolin. The bottom chord symbol is for tenor banjo.

Chords for Mandolin and Tenor Banjo

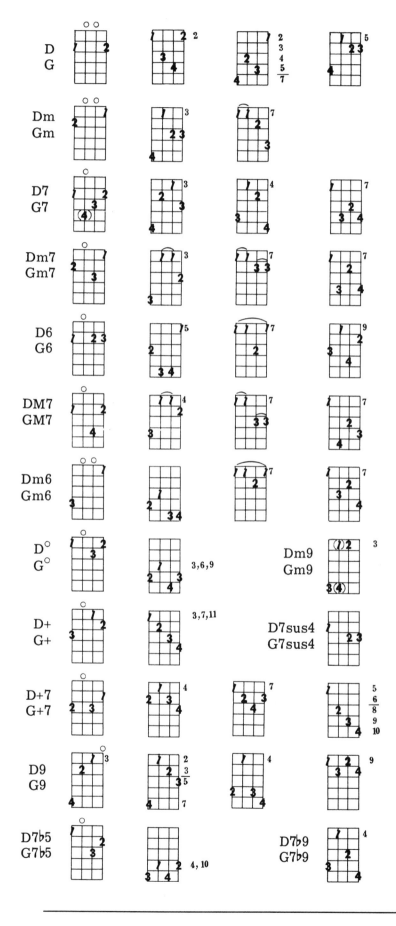

The top chord symbol next to each diagram is for the mandolin. The bottom chord symbol is for tenor banjo.

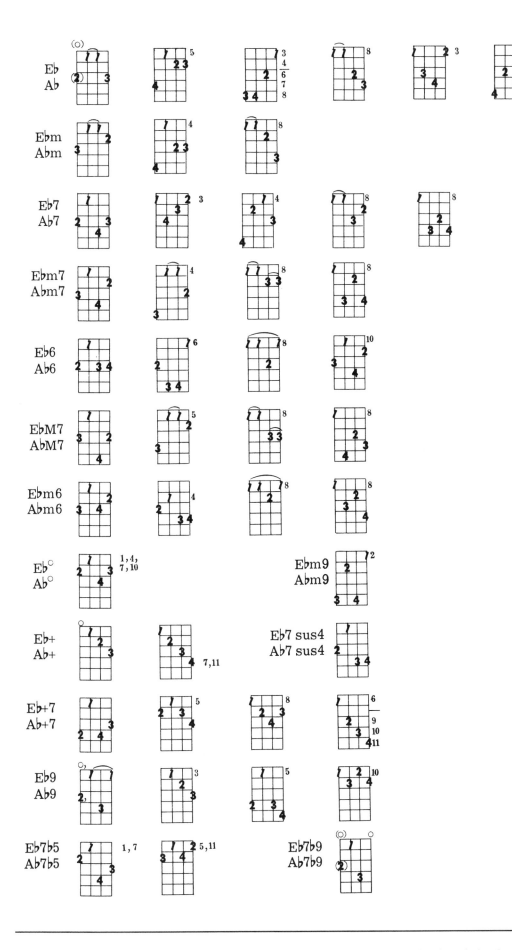

The top chord symbol next to each diagram is for the mandolin. The bottom chord symbol is for tenor banjo.

Chords for Mandolin and Tenor Banjo

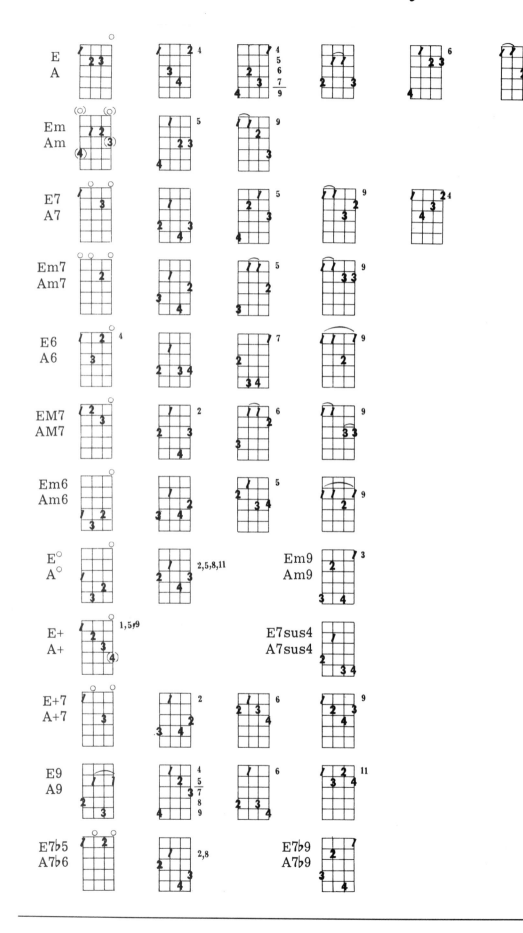

The top chord symbol next to each diagram is for the mandolin. The bottom chord symbol is for tenor banjo.

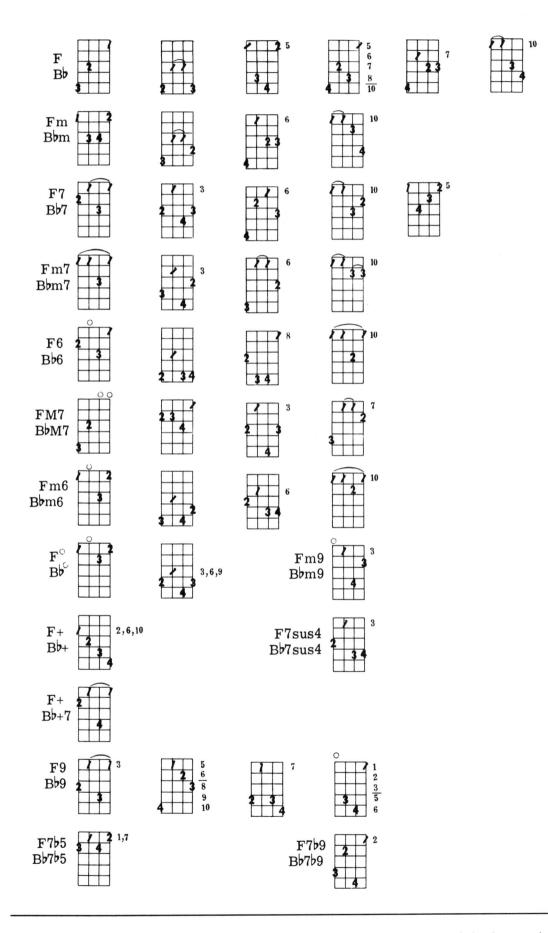

The top chord symbol next to each diagram is for the mandolin. The bottom chord symbol is for tenor banjo.

Chords for Mandolin and Tenor Banjo

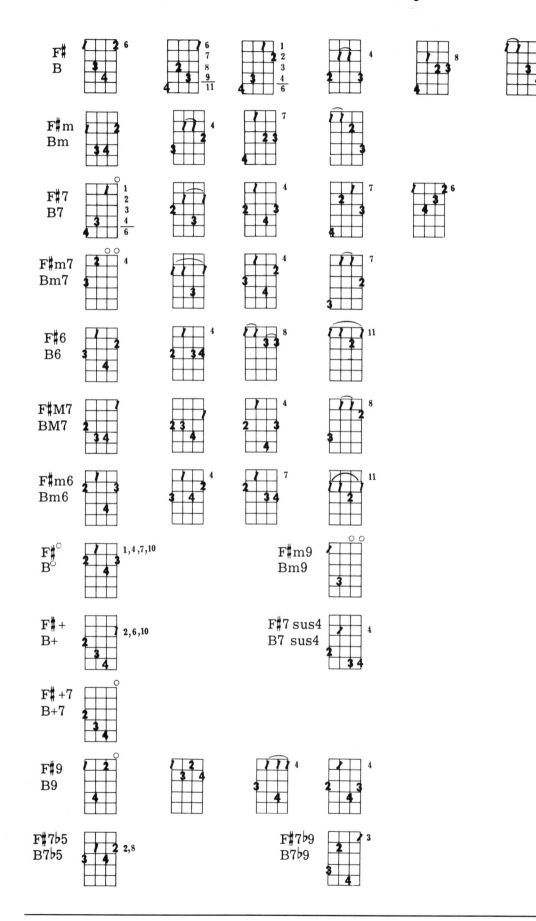

The top chord symbol next to each diagram is for the mandolin. The bottom chord symbol is for tenor banjo.

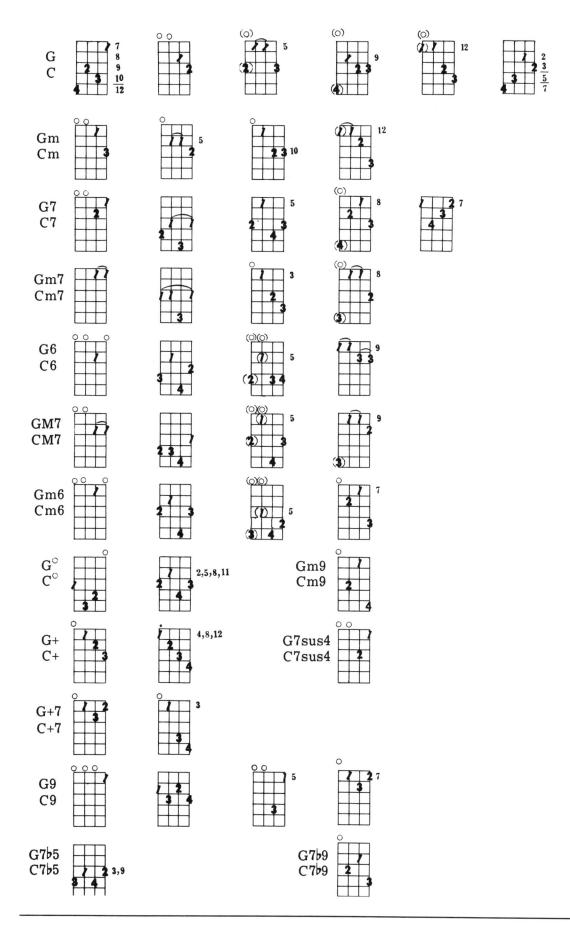

The top chord symbol next to each diagram is for the mandolin. The bottom chord symbol is for tenor banjo.

Chords for Mandolin and Tenor Banjo

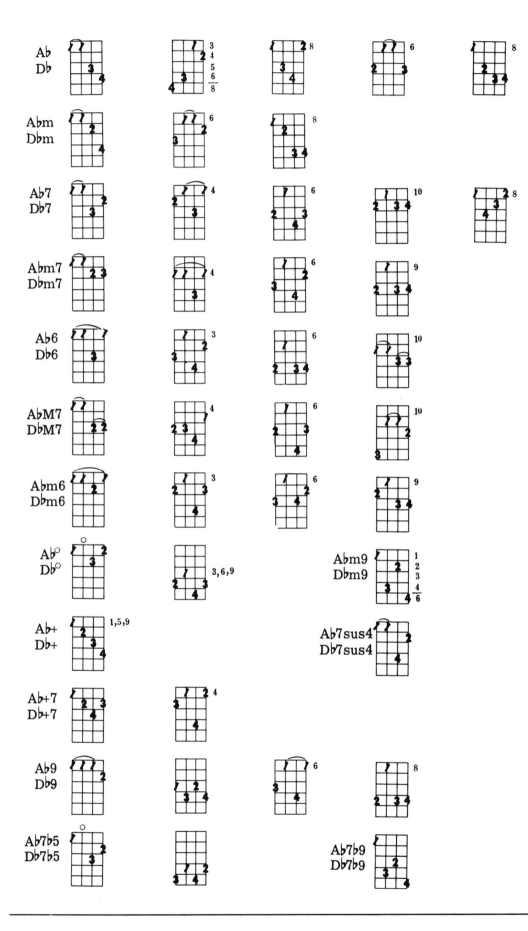

The top chord symbol next to each diagram is for the mandolin. The bottom chord symbol is for tenor banjo.

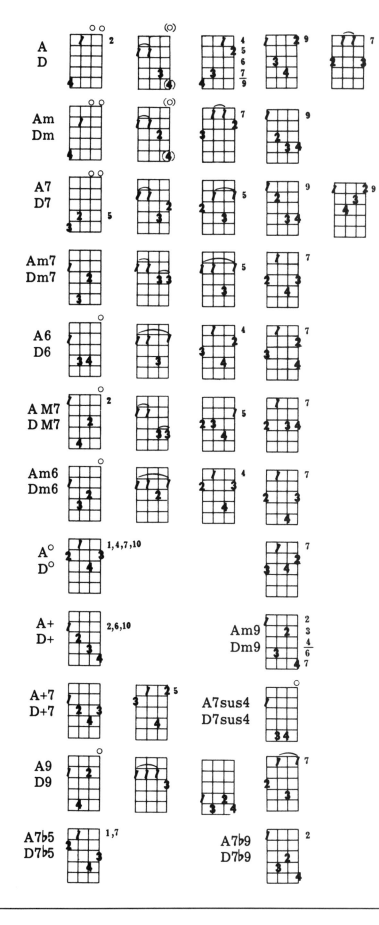

The top chord symbol next to each diagram is for the mandolin. The bottom chord symbol is for tenor banjo.

Chords for Mandolin and Tenor Banjo

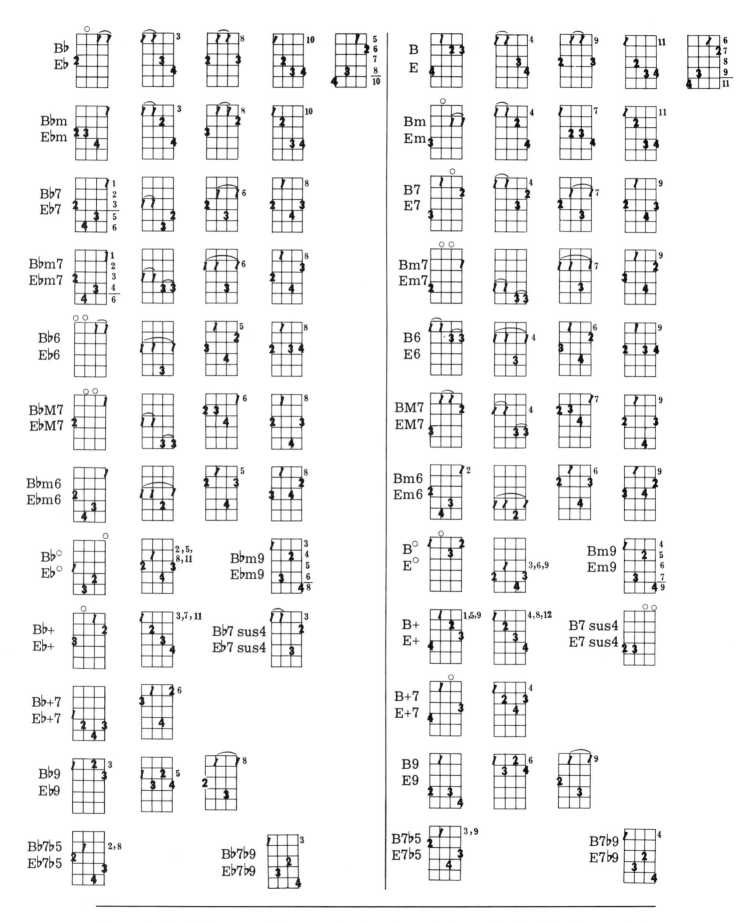

The top chord symbol next to each diagram is for the mandolin. The bottom chord symbol is for tenor banjo.

 # Book 6

Guitar Manuscript Paper

The last book in *The Guitarist's Bookshelf* provides a supply of music manuscript paper especially designed for guitarists. This is a great place to jot down new chords, riffs, or complete songs or solos. If and when you run out of any of these three types of guitar manuscript paper, you can obtain more from your local music store. Just ask for Passantino guitar manuscript paper in the style you require.

Contents

Guitar Tablature Paper

This two-line paper is designed for guitar solos of any kind. It provides a standard treble staff aligned with a guitar tablature staff. For more information on writing music for the guitar, see the section "Guitar Tablature and Notation" in *Book 2: Music Theory for Guitarists*.

Vocal/Guitar Tablature Paper

Use this three-line paper to write out songs for voice and guitar. You can add lyrics between the first and second staff, if desired. This paper is also useful for writing or arranging instrumental compositions for guitar and a solo treble instrument, such as flute, recorder, violin, clarinet, or trumpet. For more information on writing music for the guitar and other instruments, see *Book 2: Music Theory for Guitarists*.

Chord Diagram Paper

Use this type of paper to diagram chords and chord inversions. For a discussion on building and naming guitar chords, as well as information on chord diagram notation, see the section "Basic Chord Theory" in *Book 4: Guitar Chord Dictionary*.

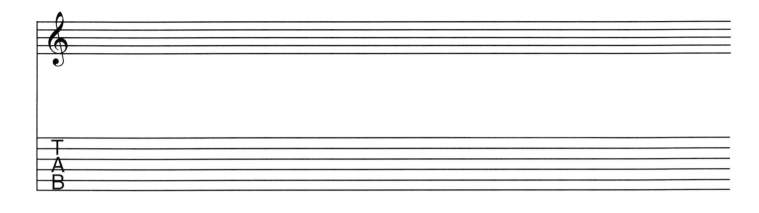

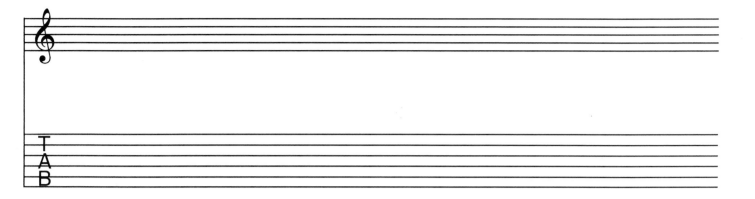

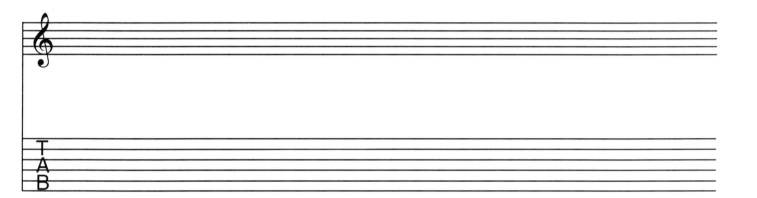

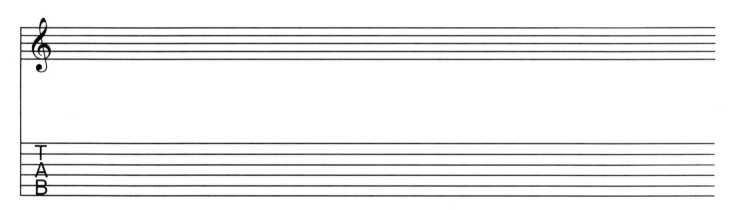

Guitar Tablature Paper

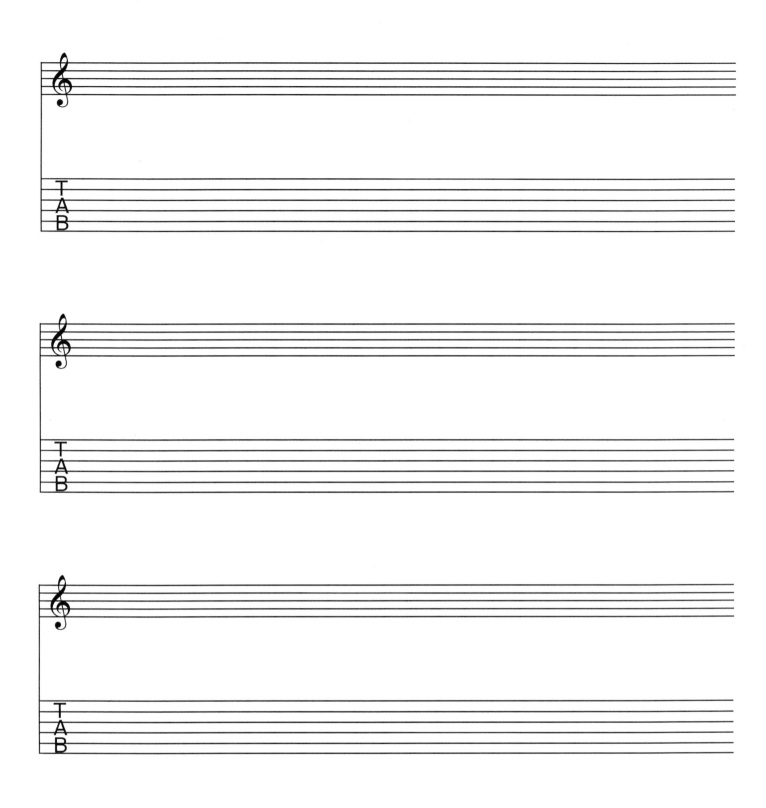

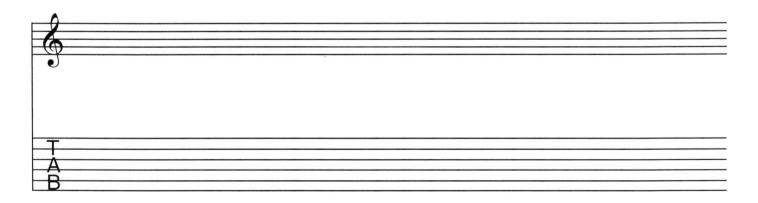

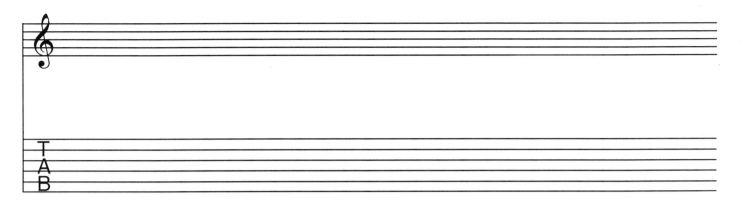

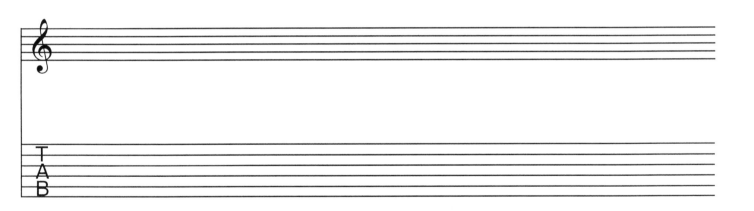

Guitar Tablature Paper

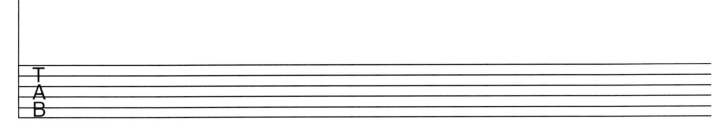

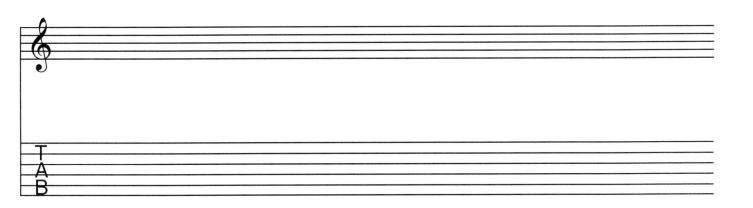

Guitar Tablature Paper

The Guitarist's Bookshelf

Guitar Tablature Paper

The Guitarist's Bookshelf

Guitar Tablature Paper

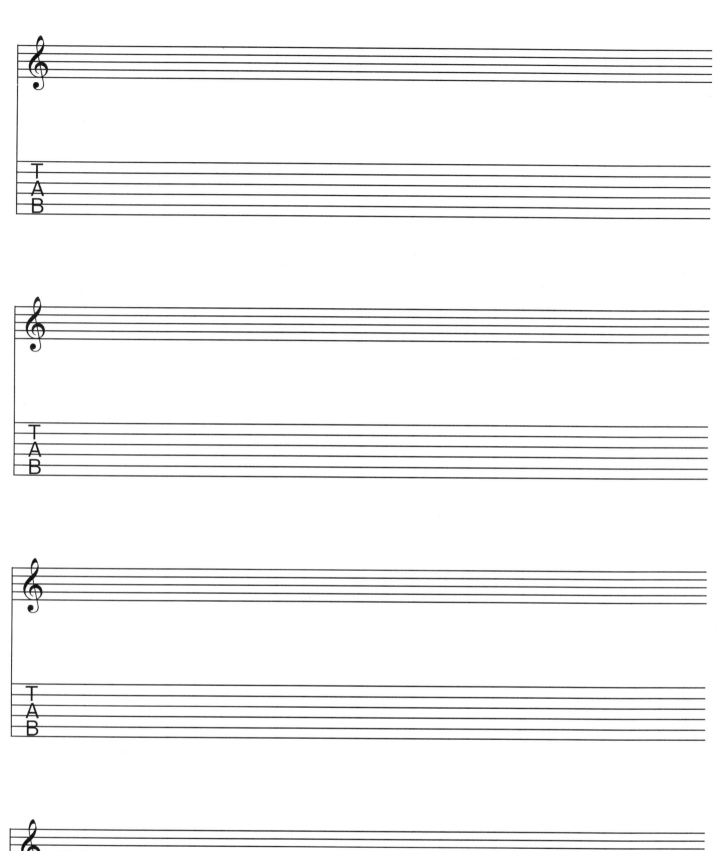

Vocal/Guitar Tablature Paper

The Guitarist's Bookshelf

Vocal/Guitar Tablature Paper

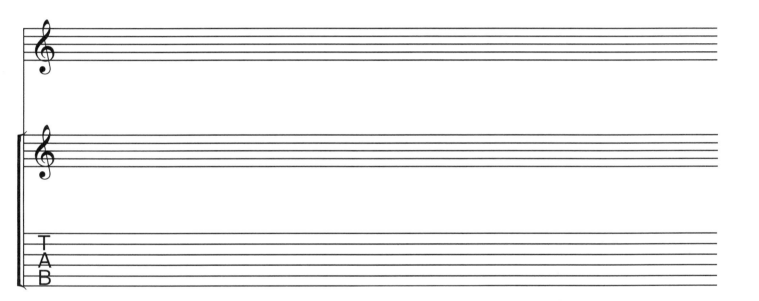

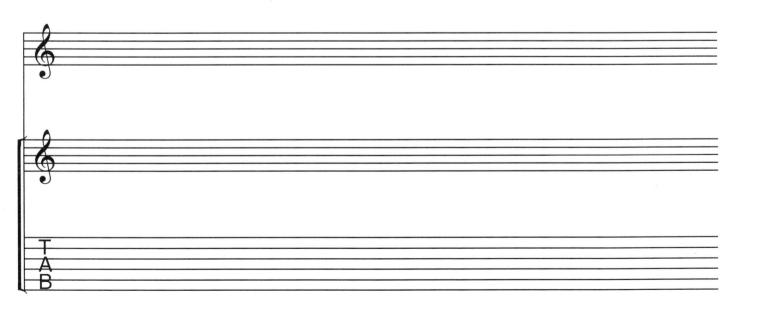

Vocal/Guitar Tablature Paper

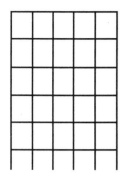
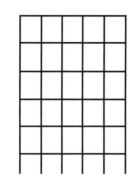
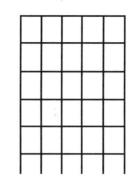
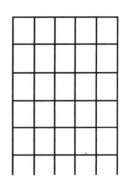

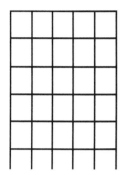
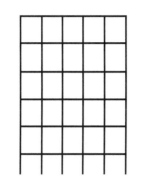

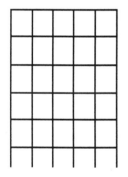
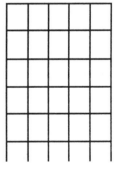

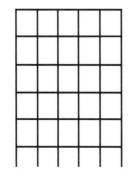
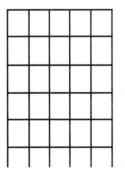

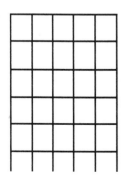

Chord Diagram Paper

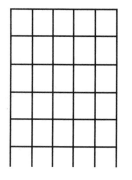
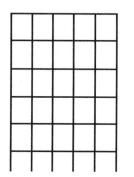
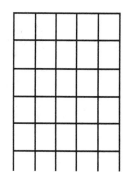
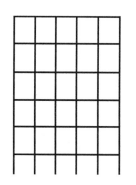
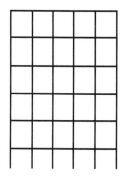
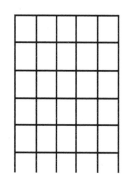
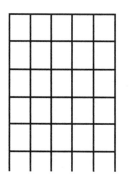
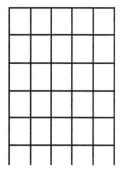

The Guitarist's Bookshelf

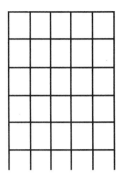
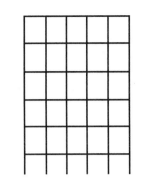
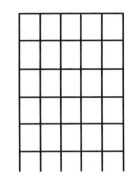
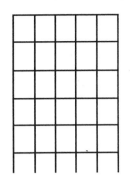

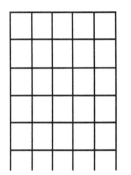
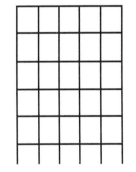
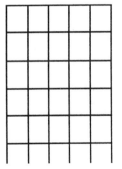
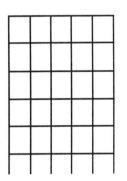

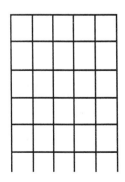
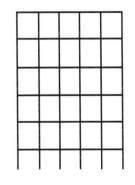

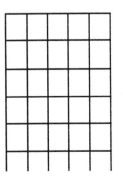

Chord Diagram Paper

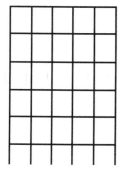
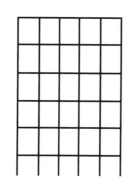
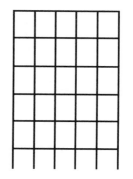
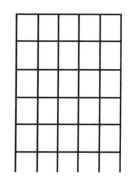

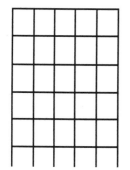
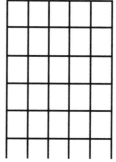
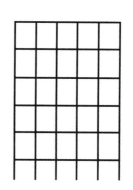
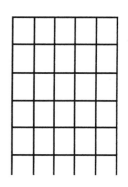

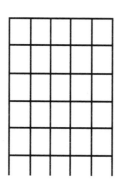
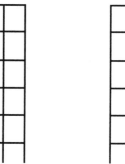
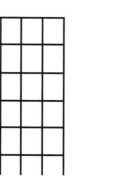

The Guitarist's Bookshelf

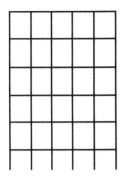
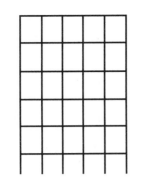
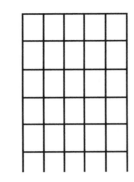
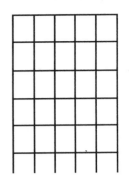

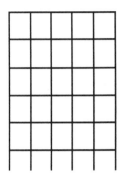
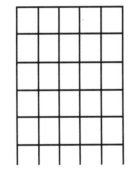
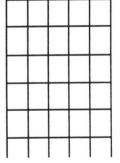
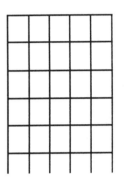

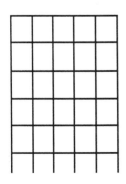
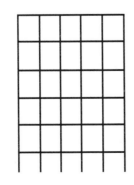
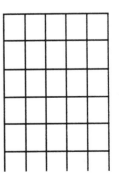

Chord Diagram Paper

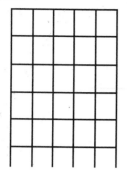
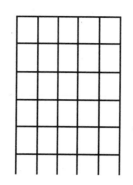
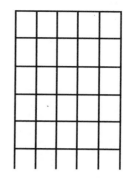
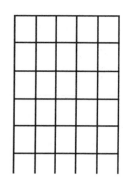

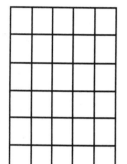
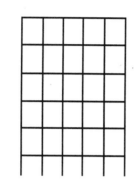
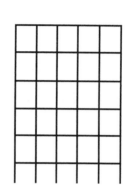
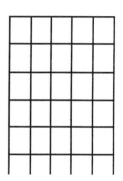

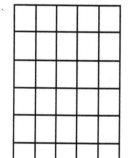
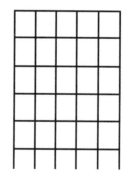

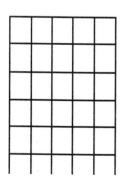
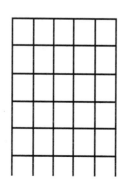
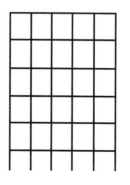
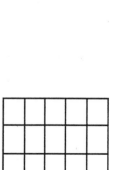

The Guitarist's Bookshelf